WHY IBB MUST NOT RULE NIGERIA...

Felix O. Vescovi

Bloomington, IN  Milton Keynes, UK

authorHOUSE

AuthorHouse™
1663 Liberty Drive, Suite 200
Bloomington, IN 47403
www.authorhouse.com
Phone: 1-800-839-8640

AuthorHouse™ UK Ltd.
500 Avebury Boulevard
Central Milton Keynes, MK9 2BE
www.authorhouse.co.uk
Phone: 08001974150

First published by AuthorHouse 12/22/05

ISBN: 1-4208-5170-5 (sc)

Printed in the United States of America
Bloomington, Indiana

This book is printed on acid-free paper.

To the true servers of Nigeria and their
'servitude'

In my course of patriotism... put money in one side and prison in the other, I will look at both indifferently. May the gods so split me if I desire money more than I fear prison or death in serving truly my country.

This book is art: a lie that tells the greater truth. 'Fiction is a marvelous shield, it's very easy to hide behind' says John Grisham, '...but when it ventures near the truth, it needs to be accurate'

As Bertrand Russell genuinely add '...without details, a book becomes jejune and uninteresting; with details, it is in danger of becoming intolerably lengthy'. With this in my mind, I have consciously endeavored to be concise while sufficiently explaining my whys in this book.

The Nigerian controversial ruling generals

Chido Nwangwu of USAfricaonline refers to this bizarre picture as the 'more you look, the less you see'... a pictorial irony and high metaphor of power friendship, betrayal and killing.

THINGS HAVE STARTED MOVING UP FOR ME AS THEY HAD had been for Babangida, though in different ways and values. I had a phone call earlier from a private television station in Lagos inviting me to present their high rated national program Give democracy a chance; a weekly program that educates millions of viewers in each live show. This week's record could be the highest live TV show in the history of Nigeria television broadcasting. It is winter in Europe and United States of America's president- W Bush is surviving all odds from his first Florida wining to his reprisal of 9/11 even after Senator Kerry had undone himself over the vague Iraq's situation and the War- President surprised the globe with a historical second victory. Months ago, British Tony Blair had labourly locked horns with the feared Tory/Lib dem parties to lead his third term in Westminster. This time, the Iraqis had just formed their first democratic government with their eyes stains with blood and their ears deafens with blasts. The axis of evil had been taciturn after Washington's groan over the quest for their holy grail- WMD. Yet Greenspam is still having nightmares why the dollar can't recover from Euro's defeat. I had planed to pass by President Mugagbe but he is too busy destroying his peoples' home since he arrived from Papá` Karol Wojtyla's lutto in Rome, an event that postponed Prince of Wale and Duchess of Cornwall's knotting nozziale. Soon after this, the German shepherd continues to guard the catholic gate.

Felix O. Vescovi

I had needed the warmth and colorful faces in Nigeria where I was born many years ago, about thirty years after Babangida was born. The program is going to be air in their Abuja studio. I will fly there but then Babangida has flown from Minna to the Federal capital city to resubmit himself to another chairmanship of the big occasion. This time, it is the National Security Watch Award ceremony. It is now quarter of Obasanjo's second term in the office, a time of no significance but when all generals though retired are cashing in on their latest massive candidateship to the post that will make them above the law and earn them many 'Hummer' jeeps and solar-system homes and of course never dry Swiss accounts. At the reception hall in the chic side of the Abuja Sheraton hotel, power-people looks down from a high red-carpeted podium on a crowded, numbered buffet tables. A female is speaking into a wireless microphone "...ladies and gentlemen please welcome his excellency, former head of Nigeria, a retired army general and now two zero, zero seven presidential candidate, President Ibrahim Baba..." non uniform claps rage the hall. As the clapping faints, a man rises to his feet from the high table. He arranges the flapping hems of his starched brocade agbada on his shoulders. His bright teeth glow from his trademark smile. A beau, the most handsome of Nigerian head of States after Buhari and Shagari. At the television studio, I'm thinking of Babangida as I sit on a chair in the dressing room having my face painted with eye shadow and blush for the preparation of the live show. I look at myself in the mirror; the tiny make-up girls did a nice job in their mascara. I am going to interview Babangida few hours from now. I sit on a single chair, a thick paper back file carrying my prepared questions rest on my laps. As I flip through the typed questions, the pressure of fame, the distortions and disruptions to life that money causes begin to form before my very eyes. In the waiting room inside the studio, cameras are setting into place but my mind is on when Babangida is to arrive from the security watch award celebration. I'm waiting. I have a lot to ask, not only from the prepared questions but also from my head. Babangida, a person the nation even the world acclaimed as the greatest 'Maradona' in Nigeria politics. He had long ago mounted a scene which had it been Hollywood, might have been scripted 'IBB the evil genius', probably accompanied with his photograph; a dracula teeth pictured in a monster form. He believes not in the medicine man, I don't mean the medical professionalism. Maybe he believes in miracles or divine inspirations that help him to cheating life and death. From where I'm sitting, I can see people scurrying inside the studio. Cameramen grab their materials to their faces. He has arrived. Dozens of double weight men in black suits clear his way into the studio. I try to look at him as a Nigerian when he walks to a prepared seat. I watch his walk, his style, the smile, and his starched brocade that reflects his physical gentleness. As I look, I'm seeing his hunger for name, fame and the power to hold it with a hiding ability that nurses an obsessive melancholy, which will be seen through this night of revelation; a necessary indulgence for he who is beyond good and evil, a demi god in a turbulent Nigerian government. He sits down in a high cultured manner with a tension of a bad life that somehow soon gives way to a gentle innocent smile. The show producer had wanted me deliver the final sword thrust to a genius who maybe 'mortally' wounded after the show. I shuffle the typed papers in my hand and resettle them on my laps. I had memorized the first question in few seconds they had milled out from a printer. I wave the unwritten questions in my head and look at the typed ones in my hand. I'm prepare for the interview but I could not tell myself at this moment that soon, what I will be asking is nothing but a terrible reminder of a man's bad life that till now he had never and can no way prove it will never happen again. His picture on the monitoring screen before the producer is still, the camera has a chest up focus. The show will start after this commercial message on war against '419'. This commercial has been on air, promoting the fight against corruption since Obasanjo was first elected into office. The effects have been nothing but one of the government's soap operas. The 9 O'clock news had just ended with the week's weather forecast. From the crew, a female, little larger than what the media recommends as beauty starts the count down

"5,4,3,2,1..." the camera's red light flash on and my face show on a screen-monitor before the producer

"Good evening viewers and welcome to another exciting edition of Give Democracy a Chance. My name is Felix, I'm your host this week and our guest, your guest today is former army general, PDP 2007 presidential candidate" the camera has the guest's fair skin face enlarge on the monitoring screen, his smile broad and sensual.

"Retired General Ibrahim B. Baba..." I turn away from the camera to face the elegant man before me

"Mr Babangida you are welcome to the program and it is nice to have you here Mr President"

"Thank you, hello viewers" he reply after a light cough to clear his throat. I'm watching the way he chooses his words in which beauty seems inspire directly by divinity. The camera zoom my face and I open the first page of my questionnaire before me. Breathing deep, I pick up the questionnaire and begin to read from the first page.

"Before she became corrupt, before she became hard to live in, before her currency fell so flat, even before all of that and beyond her failings, she was one other thing, she was our country...our Nigeria. In this definition, where will you put yourself?" He balance himself and the usual hypocrisy follows

"Nigeria is my country and I am doing what I know best doing"

"You are from Niger State?"

"Yes! A Gwari origin"

"A biographer has this vague claim you are a Yoruba?"

"Who is this biographer?"

"I was expecting confirmation" giving him a diplomatic look

"Well, any book out on this?"

"No, not that I know of, but it's rumored that there is this paternal origin linking to Ogbomosho"

"I am curious to read any book on that"

"How will you describe yourself in a sentence" he laughs and tries to answer the question but he couldn't form an instant sentence

"If your next book is going to be on Nigeria, what would be the title?"

"Nigeria of IBB"

"You are address as Doctor?" He hem

"Yes. I had to be called that incase anybody want to use book against me. In Nigeria you have to prepare for every thing. It is not only me, Igbinedion and the rest are address Doctors too"

"You have four lovely kids, Mohammed, Aisha and the rest two"

"Yes, Aminu and Halima"

"Aisha and Mohammed took their names after their paternal grand parents"

"Yes"

"Aisha's wedding was one of its kind"

"I thank Allah for her, she needed that crowd and I provided it for her"

"31 State governors, 62 senators, 69 members of the House of Representatives, over 100 former law makers"

"Yes, I live with my people"

"Aisha have grew up to a fine young promising lady"

"Yes"

"Her handsome husband…" he smiles and his teeth glow like that in a tooth past advert in a colored television.

"He is doing good"

"He paid 25,000 Naira and 31 pounds of gold to get your beautiful daughter?"

"Yes" his laughter is now like that of a spectator in 'nite of a thousand laugh' show

"Your son in-law is Abacha's nephew?" he nods for confirmation

"Babangida and Abacha?"

"Yes..." he balance himself as if he is going to say things that will finally put to rest all that had rumored between the two families

"You see, politics in this country is very complicating, I have being in it from the beginning of my time. The public says whatever they think and not what is really going. The real people in the arena know themselves and we arrange the stage. Everyone has his or her role in the theatre. Every thing is design. At times things slips and to put the stage light on again means to cut off some things or some people. My family and Abacha's family are inside the arena. So the public should just seat back and watch"

"Vice president Atiku Abubarkar ate and danced at your daughter's wedding. You are really friends"

"Yes we are when we don't have anything to fight for" he gives a twitchy look across the audience

"Now that you are both heading to the same arena in 2007"

"The most furious gladiator will survive"

"People call you Maradona and Abacha a bully. How was he able to maneuver you and took his name from the list of the officials you retired before you left office"

"He didn't. I personally allowed him to stay as I have said earlier" I'm not getting the answer. I have to move to the next question

"Your dude kid Mohammed, the polo star and the rest kids schooled or are schooling abroad?"

"Yes"

"But we have schools here"

"Well, I want them to go to good school"

"President Obasanjo definitely will side his vice in the 2007 presidential race"

"He told you that?" his question carries some seriousness of curiosity rather than of doubt

"Logically, his vice"

"Don't say what you don't know. I was with Obasanjo when he came in, in 1976. I worked with him administratively in his 1976-1979 government. I know all his secrets and tricks, so relax"

"Rumor had it that your family name has a share in Swiss watch company" the question is irritating like a skin suffering from allergy

"You never told Nigerians where you got the money from?"

"Did Obasanjo tell you where he got his Ota-farm money from? Or did Buba Marwa explained where he got his Albarka Airline's money from?"

"In 2005 Democracy Day celebration, Obasanjo in his speech outlined most things he cannot stand, among many is intimidation. In his words…" I turn to my questionnaire" '…in my age, I will rather die, all dis bad belle people'… who was he referring to?"

"When death comes, we all will die, each at his own turn"

"When Chinua Achebe did not honor his award, that was a big blow to the government?"

"Ask who is ruling. In my time, I won't worry myself about that"

"Buhari is still having his election issue in court?" he shrugs to say, that is history already. There is nothing one can do about it.

"Let talk about your junta, you promised to bring an end to human right abuse when you overthrew Buhari 27 August 1985"

"Yes I needed to justify myself of the coup and I found that appealing to the public"

"And you promised to handover in 1990 but you never did"

"I wouldn't have in 1993 if not the pressure that became too much. As I have said in other interviews, I needed Shonekan to stay there for me to rearrange, bammm! Abacha" he gesticulates the action

"Back to your SAP program of 1986, the deregulation of agriculture by abolishing marketing boards and elimination of price controls, naira devaluation and all that but it ruined our economy"

"I thought it could work"

"But you should have studied it first before implementing it"

"Study, I was a soldier I needed no study"

"You promised when you took over to abolish human abuse but State Security Decree Number 2 stayed firm in your regime, you strengthened it and that same Decree you used against trade union, student groups, journalists and many individuals"

"Look these people wouldn't let me see road"

"You upgraded Nigeria's role in the Organization of the Islamic Conference as a full member"

"Yes"

"But Nigeria is not an Islamic state. With full respect to my fellow citizens who are Muslims"

"Well I am a Muslim and I was ruling then"

"Back to April 22 1990"

"Oh my God" his remote gaze and fixed expression of unserene impassiveness send me into an unreal atmosphere which continues to repeat itself in many variations. His face dreads with memory that presents pathos on that drama with all the violent details.

"Gideon Orkar"

"Uhmm..." he tries to speak but the name before him is a ghost in a festive Halloween.

"Thank God he is gone" he manages to say

"The period he controlled the radio station in Lagos, he said the reason for his overthrown was for your dictatorial nature and pervasive corruption"

"Well that was then" the producer signal me for a commercial break. I look into the camera

"This is give democracy a chance, with me is retired General, former military head of State and the twenty O seven PDP presidential candidate. More questions and answers when we come back, don't go away" the commercial message is short, a good offer on a new improved washing powder.

"Welcome back" I face my guest.

"State Security Service (SSS), why was it necessarily to be created and took out the NSO?"

"Look I saw some radical groups coming up. I needed to set up the SSS and manage it in three heads"

"It was money consuming to create SSS and destroyed NSO but there was no deference after all in their duty"

"To the public there was no deference but to me there was. Then I was able to control the security myself"

"You scrapped the Decree Number 4?"

"Yes to have Decree Number 2 workable, with this I was able to deal with Fawehinmi, Solarin and the rest of them"

"And the media, you were not in good term with the media" he tries not to show how disgusting this question is. He might have thought not to answer the question during the silence. He seems not too bothered about the public feeling if he doesn't answer the question. At last he works out an answer with a smile - his normal trademark

"The media had always wanted to hear or know what I was doing, 'Newswatch' for instance was a pain in the butt"

"At last what happened?"

"You know it"

"When you called Shonekan in late 1993, He didn't know he was going to last only three months?"

"Well, I explained everything to him and I told Abacha to watch him but as you can imagine when you are not in the arena, it won't be exactly as you plan the stage. So you have to draw the curtain to restage before the theatre starts playing again"

"And you were in Egypt when your back watcher struck Shonekan"

"Yes, I did not want to be in the country when it will happen, so I left when it was time". This time his face is relax and carry no worry of any kind, probably thinking of rephrasing the answer or trying to change the subject entirely

"Shonekan said he gave the office to Abacha voluntarily"

"Voluntarily?" he laughs

"Who gives power up voluntarily in Nigeria? You don't really live here"

"Gideon's April 1990 coup speech reads..." I bend down to my questioning papers on the table and begin to read '...dictatorial, corrupt, drug baronish, evil man, deceitful, homo-sexually centered, prodigalistic, what else, unpatriotic ...Babangida"

"These are what we say when a soldier overthrow, it's like that. Look again what I said about Buhari"

"But Gideon went on to say..." his face flop, I could swear from his panting, he wish never to hear that name again

"...you murdered Dele Giwa, Major-General Mammman Vasta, with other officers"

"These people are dead"

"Rumor has it that you always have this intense desire to make yourself a life President and Orkar confirmed it in his coup speech"

"Anyone would like to be a life President" his reply is warm and I look at him and back to my questioning papers but something in my memory came up but I saved it for amongst the last

"What about the Sokoto caliphate, there was unclear legitimacy of the sultan then"

"Yes, that was to cause confusion within the Caliphate itself"

"Why was that necessary?"

"Just to lower its' power that was at that time a kind of big and that threatened me"

"Your close friend, back watcher Abacha was killed?"

"You know he used Viagra?"

"No, I don't know"

"See..." he lean closer to me as if it is a secret he had love me to keep. His voice narrow and his eyes swinging.

"...he used Viagra and his Indian pololos were too much for him" he concludes in sotto voce

"His death remains a mystery?"

"Mystery to some people"

"A lot of people know the real cause?"

"Of course yes" this time his tone solemn

"Abacha wanted to play the game I designed. He wanted to leave uniform then force people to accept him as the only democratic presidential candidate and that was bad" he shrug his shoulder and his face carries a betrayed emotion.

"And you were furious"

"You can bet"

"So he was gone"

"Yes, and I quickly put my cousin in there"

"Who, oh Abubakar?"

"Yes"

"But Abubakar was not the most senior officer then"

"No, Useni and others were there"

"But Useni didn't come in?"

"No, he didn't know much, I kept him in a distance"

"In a hard time like that, the infamous quiet cousin was not the right choice"

"For me he was. I was there with him anyway" I'm trying to imagine the million viewers before their TV sets. I could hear voices shouting, yelling and I can hear families squabbling

"You funds Islamisation in northern Nigeria"

"Yes, the trouble was to destabilize Obasanjo and his vice"

"Has this Islamic legal system come to stay?"

"No doubt about that"

"President Obasanjo is your friend, why doing this to him" he shakes his head lightly and lost what he was to say. I let it pass. I might come back for it, later, much more later

"In your era. You changed members of your government frequently"

"That was the rule of the game, don't let one stay too long or else he knows more about you...then you gone"

"Even your second man Ukiwe?"

"Yeah, he was calm but there was something I couldn't understand about him"

"So you decided to change him?"

"Yes! It took me time to get a substitute. I needed a weak 'yes sir' man in that place and Aikhomu fitted in the place. I put Aikhomu there as a figure head so as to shot up the southerners who were saying the government was full of the northerners"

"How will you describe Nigeria religious status?"

"Nigeria is a free country with different religious beliefs"

"But you made her a member of OIC? I now this is a repeat question but I just can't understand why"

"Oh yeah, then I was ruling nothing more"

"The 12.4 billion dollars 1st gulf war oil windfall"

"It was used"

"For what?"

"It is in our record, I can't remember all of that now"

"What about the People's Bank of Nigeria"

"Oh that was a bait to bridle Tai Solarin"

"You gave money to defense and police projects more than education, health or agriculture?" he ridicule me with his look and I need not to hear what is to follow

"You were always going to abroad for medical treatment, like your famous France orthopedic surgery"

"I was ill"

"Does that mean you couldn't treat yourself here in the country"

"Obviously there were no good hospitals"

"And you were putting more money into defense and police when there are no good hospitals"

"That was my area of interest"

"What about the people you were governing, you never consider their own interest?"

"Not as much as I do about my security and means to stay in power"

"What about the Okigbo panel"

"What about it?"

"You did not appear"

"No!"

"And the 12.4 billion oil money?"

"I said it earlier, it was used"

"How?" his frustration over the question is like that of an airline passenger in Muritala Mohammed airport without a confirmed seat

"Fawehinmi said you killed Dele Giwa"

"He brought papers upon papers but here in this country who look at papers?"

"You avoided the Oputa panel, will you appear before any other panel now"

"Yes, I know how to free myself anyway"

"You live in a 50 room home"

"Yes, it is a hilltop mansion"

"A lot of people are saying they will never vote for you if you happen to contest in the 2007 presidential election"

"I will get the necessary vote to rule this country without any disturbance. I will be given the vote I need when the time comes"

"But how, hence people are saying they will not vote for you"

"Look you talking as if you are hearing of me for the first time, don't forget history so soon"

"I don't see how you are answering the question of how do you think you will win if nobody is voting for you"

"Don't stress yourself. The people will vote but it is the electoral commission that will announce the winner"

"And you spend 40 billion naira in power transition program but power you never give"

"Sincerely I had never wanted to handover, that is why I was using option A4 as a delay tactics. After June 12, I knew I couldn't stay. So I have to organize Shonekan to stay for some time"

"He indeed accepted"

"Yes he did, the original deal was he will be my vice when I becomes civilian president, so when the whole thing did turned out bad"

"He now went in there still part of a pregnant deal"

"That was it"

"In your time, the army, defense were well feed but the air force was like a church rat"

"Yeah, my dream was to dissolve the air force but then my close pal Ibrahim Alfa was the chief of Air Staff. So I left it running for his sake but with nothing"

"Why for Alfa's sake?"

"Oh, he was my friend and he helped me in the coup when I struck Buhari. He took good care of Idiagbon. He helped me to vote him to go to Mecca and he went with him"

"Alfa was with Idiagbon in Mecca when you struck"

"It was planned he monitored the strong man over there"

"Why did you organize Idiagbon to be away before you strike?"

"He was a strong man, it was better for us he was not there"

"If Idiagbon was present, you wouldn't have succeeded?"

"That was why he had to be away"

"Then why did the air force suffered, knowing that the head of the air force helped you?"

"Yes, Mamman Vatsa was to use the air force to overthrow me.

So I had to make sure there were no materials there that could help any future idea like that of Vatsa"

"We hear this information..." he is not following what I'm saying, a picture from the screen showing his military uniform speech takes his attention

"...thanks to John Fashanu that Bob Minto admitted that 450 billion naira debt buy-back was arranged with him by your government"

"Don't mind that loud white mouth, he can't keep secrets"

"Abiola..."I could read his high interest on his face before I finish my sentence

"He was my friend"

"Friend?"

"Yes, you surprise?"

"A bit"

"Don't be, he was my friend, we had known each other for a very long time. He supported me. He financed my coup against Buhari"

"Why?"

"Buhari and Idiagbon said the newspaper should be using home made materials so when Abiola continued to import newsprint materials Buhari seized them. After that incident Abiola was no longer in good term with

18

them and when his help was needed to finance the coup, he had a good reason to assist"

"Obasanjo have a commission to investigate human rights abuse"

"I know that"

"He is more on Abacha, what about you. Rumor has it that you did lot of killings, why is Obasanjo commission not investigating you?"

"You should ask Obasanjo this question"

"Do you know why you are not included in the commission's list"

"I know for sure"

"Then tell the nation"

"You see I gave a critical support to Obasanjo in his both term presidential campaign. I gave him a lot of money, how do you expect him now to bite the finger that feed him?"

"Obasanjo is having your ex aids like Aliyu Muhammed, T. Danjuma in his cabinet"

"It doesn't happened by chance, I pushed my boys in there to give me feedback continuously"

"You often quote the 1910's 'A man for all reasons' of The United States of America president; Theodore Roosevelt"

"I love the concept"

"There is this, your address to the nation on the 26th of June 1993, let me take a part of the speech" a video switch on and Babangida in khaki is speaking '... Nigeria has come along since this administration assumed power and leadership about Eight years ago. In the attempt to grapple with the critical and monumental problems and challenges of national existence

and social progress, this administration inaugurated and pursued sound and justifiable policies and programs of reforms. This policies and programs have touched virtually all aspects of our national life...economy, political process, social structure, external relations, bureaucracy and even the family system...' I raise my head from the questionnaire

"If you will be sincere with yourself and to your Nation, looking back now how will you reconfirm this words"

"I am not sure"

"What you promised Nigeria in 1985 was economic reconstruction, social justice and self-reliance. Would you say you kept your promise in eight years"

"I was still working on those promises till 1993"

"You said in an interview with the 'Daily champion' that only God can stop you from being the president in 2007"

"If that is what you read, they wrote that themselves. I said when God ordained someone in a position, nobody can stop him, except God Himself don't want him"

"The message is very clear. In this case you were referring to who"

"Myself"

"You meant what you said?"

"Yes"

"Again what makes you so confident about Nigerian voters...the public poll is very, very unfavorable to you"

"I am not saying what I don't know, we are in 2006, and the vote of 2007 has been cast"

"And you already know the winner"

"Obviously"

"Frankly, those supporting you on this presidential race are your friends and people you had given help and money. The majority, the overwhelming Nigerians, which is the sovereign is saying no to your coming back. If there should be a referendum, a clear and fair public opinion conducted on your presidential aspiration and say about 80% of the country's population vote against you, will you step down from the race?" nervousness is crawling into his face. It is very hard to hide agitation now.

"No, I will not step down"

"Let's move back to 1993"

"You said you explained to Shonekan when you called him in"

"Not the 90 days stay anyway"

"And you were in Egypt when your man struck Shonekan"

"Yes, I didn't want to be in the country when it will happen, so I left when it was time I said that before"

"Yeah right" I look to my papers

"Lets go over this again" he agrees with a nod and look away at the audience

"Gideon's 1990 coup speech reads" I pick up the page I had read before

"...'dictatorial, corrupt, drug baronish, evil man, deceitful, homosexually centered..." I stopped and breathed.

"...prodigalistic, unpatriotic...Babangida" finally I stop taking a breath and to look at his face for reaction, I'm seeing nothing

21

"I have told you how it works"

"That means they are not true?"

"I am not saying that, rather"

"Gideon went on...'the murderer of Dele Giwa, Major-General Mamman Vasta, with other officers..."

"A lot of people say that"

"If a lot of people say that and does that makes it true or false?" silence

"Don't you think it is appropriate as a human right defender as you claim to investigate these accusations"

"Who will do the investigation?"

"The government"

"Forget that" he concludes in a ridiculing tone

"The Kano riot thing, what was it?"

"Just to lower Obasanjo's power"

"In all this facts why is the government not probing, investigating you?"

"Investigate?"

"Yes, why is the government not doing anything to all this horrendous facts"

"Who is the government?" he swallows heavy saliva, a way of delaying his reply or an excuse to dodge the question. I notice that and I decide to take the trap to further questioning. I will not forget"

"In December 2002 your presented your book; 'IBB a heritage reform'"

"Yes"

"This is from your speech, '...this 'book launch' may not necessarily be a mere ceremony to celebrate the past as embodied in the reforms, which were undertaken in the 1985-1993, incidentally period 'the IBB years' as that period has come to be popularly referred to are easily the most discussed years in the Nigeria's recent history...' Why did you think is the most discussed years in Nigeria's recent history?"

"People are still talking about it"

"I know"

"A lot happened in that period. It is very remarkable because it was a period the past politics came along and it became the period the future politics will go"

"Negatively or positively"

"Either way, people are still talking about it"

"This connects me to your favorite President Roosevelt words"

"A man for all reasons?"

"Yes..." As soon as he quote the Roosevelt title again, it is obvious he likes to be the Emperor in the Amphitheatre, rejoicing in the blood that flow from the gladiatorial combat and resentful with a psychological drama with all the violent details.

"You said to celebrate in the reforms, what is it to celebrate in these your past?"

"A lot will be remembered"

"I asked to celebrate"

"I see it the same"

"Your speech continued…'ten years after 'The IBB years', it is perhaps an appropriate time for the scholarship and Journalism to begin to provide better insight into the objective motives and motivations of our choice of the reforms, which we undertook at that time'… You want to put more light on that?" It seems the question is not clear. Let me try to rephrase it

"How do you mean? Are you saying that the scholars and the media had started seeing good in your reforms or they should try to see good in it"

"They should try to see good in it"

"Could this be a campaign or lobby?"

"Yes! Now that I am heading towards candidateship"

"The scholars and media have been saying that your reform was a bad one. Is it not time you accept it that your reform was really bad and take some responsibility that is required of a good leader"

"I don't want to accept that my reform was bad"

"Even when it was bad"

"It was not bad"

"You confirmed in your book launch speech that the change of government you led in August 1995…"

"85" he corrects

"Oh sorry, in 1985. You said it was not of personal reasons but to safe guard our fundamental values"

"That is right"

"And you repeated this thereafter in several other landmark speeches"

"Yes"

"Looking at these promises and the fulfillment, if you want to conduct public opinion polls on facts, do you think you will pass?"

"Sincerely I don't think I will, but I know my ways"

"Now, knowing truly from your heart that the Nigerian people except these your friends you help up there don't want you to rule them again, why are you still dragging yourself by all means to rule"

"But I want to rule"

"Irrespective of people's opinion"

"Absolutely"

"Is this patriotism?"

"I think it more of ambition"

"In the expense of the whole nation"

"You appealed to Nigerians to judge every regime or administration on the basis of its reforming ideals or lack of such ideas. During and after your period, majority of Nigerians have being judging your idea bad and your reforms disastrous to the nation"

"I know"

"This will affect you in your candidateship"

"The NEC people are not going to look at that"

"NEC?"

"The Nigeria Electoral Commission and the other guys in Abuja don't look at this thing you are worrying about"

"You confirmed that there is no doubt the situation in the country today needs more work in reforming the political, economy and improving the quality of life of our people and the communities"

"Yes that is very much true"

"Statistic from scholars and media and the present government says the present problem of Nigeria came up due to your bad rule worsened by the period of your back watcher Abacha"

"Who said that?"

"Obasanjo said the country was so bad that his two terms in office will not produce much because of the way you and your successor ruined the country"

"What a fine way to dodge his failure" He reply laughing

"It is very interesting when you talked about leadership. This is from you on leadership...'only leadership which fully understand the reciprocal complexity of the relationship between the supremacy of civilian authority and the concomitant support base for the modern State-system provided by the military are best suited to upright and sustain our democracy" he is shaking his head

"When you talked about your future challenge, you said there is doubt whether any of you can afford to be in retirement"

"Yes I said that"

"We... who are you referring to as we. The ten or there about who rotates, circle and re-recycle power from hand to hand?"

"You ask intelligent questions, you should know by now what I mean"

"Know what?"

"Know the answer of what I mean by 'we'"

"Okay, if ten of you don't leave there for young ideas, how do you think things will work"

"We will work it just as things are going"

"People with bright ideas are there, and you know it, you don't give them a chance"

"You think we don't have ideas?"

"But nothing seems working with your ideas"

"Look if I see who have ideas, I normally call him to work for me"

"They work for you?"

"Yes, this Nigerian from US, UK and other places"

"But you dictate to these guys"

"They work under me, their ideas has to be the way I want it"

"If he insist to continues his real idea that doesn't favor you?"

"He leaves immediately"

"He leaves with his better idea?"

"You funny, no one have a better idea than his master. I have never hard this before". I'm embarrassed with his laughter now

"Now as a civilian, you keep acknowledging your regime"

"I need to"

"You won the Nigeria Person of the year 2004"

"Yeah, this Nigeria in Diaspora Organization needed some money and they came up with that, so I gave them the money. The idea is one of the ways I am using to rebuild my reputation in the public"

"And it works?"

"To some extent it helps in my public appearance"

"In 1998 your wife Maryam was awarded woman of the year by the 'New Nigerian'" he blinks his eyes trying to get what I'm saying if it's a question or just a confirmed statement. I decide not to bother him with that kind of question again. I have something else on Maryam to try on but that will be later, far later I will ask him of his wife's award of the international recognition by the Harlem Women Committee of the USA.

"Is it true you single handedly over turned and disarmed Lt. Colonel Buka Suka Dimka coup that killed the then head of State Muritala Mohammed?"

"Dimka was my friend, he knew me very well. So they sent me to him where he took hold of the radio station in Lagos and did severe harm to the Dodan barracks".

"They sent you to him"

"When I got there, he didn't believe I would set him up. When he saw me he never thought of betrayal so he let me in"

"And that was it?"

"Yes that was it"

"You acclaim yourself as a human right and democracy defender?"

"That is correct"

"Let us take the human right issue first"

"There are no evidences of your human right activities Decree Number 2 you left in place when you came in 1985 is a good example"

"Well..." he want to talk but an instant memory block him for some seconds

"*...human rights were so abused that the then president of The United States Ronald Reagan has to send you volumes of books on human rights*"

"*I thought the books were for solidarity reason*"

"*Obviously it was an irony. Human rights was what the white house wished for Nigeria at that period*"

"*I couldn't get that message then*"

"*Reagan said he had confident in you to bring Nigeria back to her potentials but you failed him*"

"*I am owning no apology*"

"*You were called president*"

"*Yes*"

"*A president in this term is an elected head of a republican state*"

"*Well I have never looked up the word president in the dictionary*"

"*Why all the names and titles*"

"*I was to rule beyond 1993, I was to leave my camouflage uniform and come straight as a full president... I had wanted people to get use to me as a president before my real presidency, just like Rawlings*"

"*Rawlings is an apple in the eyes of the Ghanaians*"

"*I know*"

"*Clear this again, the changes in your officers late 19989...Ukiwe for Aikhomu and many ministers, Bali and others*"

"*This change made me more powerful than ever*"

"*You formed two parties NRC and SDP?*"

"*Yes*"

"Heading towards democracy, anybody would had had the freedom to form as many parties as possible"

"If they were too many I could not have controlled them and fix them into my plans"

"Democratically, people have right to form any party"

"But not with me. I was playing a written theatre and I needed to coordinate the stage"

"That was not a democratic spirit"

"In my democracy you have to work things in your favor not that of the people. You see Obasanjo made a deal with the Abacha's family on their embezzled money"

"Yes"

"You see that is how we work"

"But this is on the expense of the nation, the poor citizens"

"Life is a price, someone at a point or another has to pay"

"The better life program..."

"Yes?"

"How did it go?"

"That was my wife's. I don't know anything about it"

"A lot of money was spend on the program by your regime but nothing today tells such a program ever existed"

"My wife"

"And you set up the People's Bank of Nigeria which in real sense had never be a people's bank"

"Just to short up some people as I have said in my many interviews, that was to show I was doing something for the poor"

"The wide gap between the rich and the poor in your period was a great alarm"

"I don't know how many people that were rich or poor, I never counted them"

"How many people...I mean the population of this country"

"Uhmm..." he looks at me then the camera

"...I didn't know how many people the country had then"

"Now?"

"I think is about 112 million"

"I can see why your period will remain the talk able in recent history" he subdues a smile and looks straight to the camera

"If you don't know how many people in the country you ruled or trying to rule again, how on earth will you govern as the public expected. You can never be a good ruler when you don't know how many people you rule"

"We will see to that"

"In your first year in power, you declared National Economic Emergency?"

"That was our only option then"

"Now, I mean today you can look back and see alternative option"

"Yes but I have to continue to defend that option"

"But that is not helping the nation"

"It is helping me"

"Back to the 1990 coup, there were a lot of civilians involved especially in financing. Was that not a sign that the people were tired of you as a military president?"

"It was a sign"

"And you had the intension to continues"

"Yes"

"Why is it that in your speeches or interviews, you hardly comments on the June 12 election annulment"

"Nothing to talk about. It was an incident that shaken me more than the 1990 coup"

"How?"

"I survived the coup but couldn't survive the June 12 issue"

"You deprived someone of his right"

"Look that episode forced me out of office. What else you want me to talk about?"

"Feel sorry about it, apologize, do something, show remorse"

"Look let me tell you something you probably don't know about the June 12"

"Okay"

"Only the Nigerian public felt aggrieved about the annulment, all other people up there making mouths now all benefited from it"

"Only those mouth making people up there benefited from it but what about the 19 out of 30 states that voted for a man to represent them. That 80% of voters you denied their rights"

"Well..."

"Well nothing" my interruption is slow but purposeful

"This is give democracy a chance and here with me is IBB, viewers you can call to contribute to the program and ask questions or give your opinion on Nigeria situations. The number to call is now on your screen double eight one, six four four three seven two. The call is 10 naira per minute plus the network charge. IBB live on give democracy a chance right after the break. Don't go away" the commercial takes forty seconds

"Welcome back" I flip a page in my questionnaire

"When you were asked about the rumor of your presidential candidateship in 2007, you said if God ordains one for something, nobody can stop it..."

"Yes"

"Does this mean no one is going to stop you from being Obasanjo successor?"

"I said this thing in English and I think is very simple to understand"

"You accused the Obasanjo's government as that of means and not o ideas"

"Yes"

"You said government is too important to be left in the hands of novice"

"Yes that is correct"

"Who will you classify as the expects to handle the important government"

"We the usual players"

"I guess your 'we' includes you Mr Babangida?"

"That is right"

"Your junta was a bad one. A public poll can confirm that. Since you left the dictatorship, you never handle any public office. You never represented this country in any form, then what makes you among the experts or the very expert the country's government should be left in your hand?" it is getting harder for him to calm, sweats forming on his fore head. His white handkerchief wipes the mounting sweat continuously

"This bring us to your educational background and political experience before you came to power" but another question from my memory comes up again and I decides to ask the question right away

"In Nigeria political personalities, who is your 'Idol'"

"Zik, Azikiwe represented compromise for the overall interest and unity of the country"

"The changes you made in late 1989, made you more powerful?"

"Absolutely"

"Does this power helped in the formation of the two political parties-NRC and SDP"

"Yes"

"How did people reacted, I mean the civilians to this"

"They were not expecting it but since was okay for the election to go on, they didn't care how many parties I formed"

"They were really tired of the green uniform" he laugh

"So they agreed on whatever you said then?"

"Yes... you remember I said if there were too much parties, I can't see or control them"

"But it was democracy and the interest of the people and not yours"

"I understand you but here in Nigeria that is not how it works, you are bringing this western equality here"

"Is that not what the loving Nigerians deserve?"

"Well..."

"I am not seeing any democratic spirit if you keep defending all this that happened"

"No, It's not a matter of defending"

"About what then? About winning election by all means" he didn't answer. I decide to go to another question without looking at the questioning papers

"You said Obasanjo made a deal with Abacha's family about the embezzled money"

"Yes?"

"What is your feeling about that?"

"That is how it works here"

"But it's all working in the expense of the poor citizens"

"Life is a price, someone at a point or another has to pay for it"

"This better life program..." I look my questioning paper

"That was my wife... I don't know much about that"

"And you set up people's Bank of Nigeria that in real sense had never be a people's bank"

"You see, the people that sold the idea to me just like the SAP thing told me it was going to work"

"But it didn't work"

"I know, but I was able to convinced the public I was doing something for the poor"

"In the Nigeria political personalities you said Zik is your idol?"

"Yes he is, Azikiwe I repeat represented compromise for the overall interest of the nation"

"How did you think Wole Soyinka will react to your respond- only God could stop you being the president when he requested an apology on June 12"

"He wants to start making mouth"

"What about the Methodist prelate Mr Sunday Mbang?"

"One of the guys I gave some pack of change, you see at times they don't do their jobs and in the case of this Mr Sunday, he was internecine". Phone begins to ring

"Hello?"

"Hello..." the incoming voice rattles through the phone speaker

"Hello and welcome to the program, your name please and where you calling from"

"My name is Sahid Mammud from Koko- Kebbi state"

"Okay Mr Mammud your question"

"I am sorry I don't have a question right now but you may allow me a few seconds to express my feeling as a citizen of this country hence the issue is about that"

"You have right to it Mr Mammud go ahead"

"Thank you. About the coming 2007 presidential election, Nigeria is faced with little or no choice about Babangida. But the reason to believe

and say Mr Babangida is a wrong choice is very simple...For what he has done, his record and his ways he continues to do things... if we as a nation seek a country that its' leader must not be emulated, then Babangida should go ahead. If we seek a leader who live shamelessly in a 50 room solar home while millions of his citizens sleeps in a palm leaves houses around the nation, then he is the one. If we are hoping to have school closure and unemployment, sending our youths away to become nuisance and beggars and prostitutes in foreign lands, then let him Babangida go in there. But if what we need is progress and real democracy, then Babangida should sit down far away from the arena and lean how to be human and patriotic before showing his face in the public. Thank you for the time and God help Nigeria"

"Thank you Mr Mammud". I turn to him, our guest

"Still on the 2007 election. In your acceptance speech of September 01 2004, you said quote '...if we have to use the letter bomb again you bet that we will', ... was that a true confession you murdered Dele Giwa and now a threat?"

"The message is very clear or not?"

"It is" I look at my questioning papers and remember another question

"Still on the September 2004 acceptance speech, you were talking about the apology requested for June 12 ...this is how you put it '...people say I should apologize for June but what better apology is there than Olusegun Obasanjo. I worked very hard to see that he was made president. I picked him up from the prison, dusted him and place him on a white horse. I *ordered my boys to guard him as he rode to Aso-Rock...' so Obasanjo was not voted in there, you placed him?"*

"Yes I did"

"Then Obasanjo in Aso -Rock is democratically illegitimate"

"Well..."

"Hello" a phone interrupts

"Hello"

"Hi Felix"

"Hello there, name and where you calling from"

"I'm Bello Tafa from Kumo in Gombe"

"Thanks for calling, your contribution please"

"You see the obvious reason why Mr Babangida shouldn't be there or in the Nigeria political scenes is very simple. You see he makes all things illegal"

"I don't make things illegal, I make them simple" Mr Babangida snap

"Simple for who? The people want to vote for a president and not you dusting a prisoner into Aso-Rock. I will say Obasanjo presidency is illegitimate hence you put him there and not the Nigerian voters"

"Thank you Tafa" I turn to the guest

"Your words continued in the September 2004 speech '...as a general, I yielded for the first time in my career, evil forces surrounded me that faithful mouth of June 1993 and I gave way. I would have sacrificed myself to stop the forces if that would have been sufficient but upon careful examination I came to the sad conclusion that the sacrifice of myself would have plunged

our country into a second civil war, a war that would have nailed Nigeria's coffin... I did so with the realization that I would be back to finish the job I began in 1985'...". A phone call interrupts. I try to continue but the ringing persist

"Hello"

"Hello" *a cracking voice comes from the phone speaker*

"Hello. You are live with give democracy a chance. Your name and where are you calling from"

"I i i i Ossskpa..." *the cracking voice becomes inaudible*

"Who... we can't hear you"

"Ussss Benn..." *it was a man but his words are inaudible*

"Okay... I am afraid we can't hear you and it is a pity our technical crew effort can't help the situation"

"Hello"

"Hello" *the voice insists*

"Can you hear me now?" *the line clears*

"Crystal clear"

"Okay, I was saying..."

"We didn't get your name and where you are calling from"

"Oh sorry"

"No problems, please tell us your name"

"I am Osakpamwan"

"And where is Osakpamwan calling from"

"From Benin, Edo state"

"Right go ahead and make your contribution to the issue"

"Yes, listening to the last part of Mr Babangida speech you quoted, I just want to say that the president we need as a nation is the president that yields to his people and not that who never, except once in his life with..." the phone piece cracks against the receiver and a busy tone follows. I turn to my guest for this question

"You said you left in 1993 just to come back?"

"Yes"

"Now you are the PDP nominee for the 2007 president election"

"Yes"

"Adisa, Alex Akinyele, David mark, Bode Gorge, Nas, Shagaya, Wole Soyinka, Arthur Nzeribe calls themselves the Babangida boys"

"Yes, they are my boys"

"Your boys"

"Are you surprised?"

"A kind of but I should know we are in Nigeria". He smiles

"And this Akinyele vowed to die for you?"

"That's it"

"How many, how much favor is he expecting from you?"

"He knows I give a lot and protect those who obeys me, he is a very wise man"

"In the same September acceptance speech, you said '...I swallowed insults. I knew that at the right time I would be back to redeem my name... to my detractors, I say be afraid, be very afraid for IBB is on the way"

"That is what I said and that is it"

"Is that a threat or intimidation?"

"It is what it is"

"Now let hear Idowu from Owo, Ondo. Idowu hello" I press the hold button on the phone but a busy tone comes up

"Hello? We lost that" I will pick another call

"Hello"

"Hello, my name is Bisi Olaguju from Abeokula"

"Your contribution please"

"Mr Babangida sounds undemocratic if he still confirms these uniform speeches and stand by them. I don't see any reason why he should ask me for a vote...he's still going there to torture people and..." he stops but to continues

"...Democracy is about discussing and balancing differences" he hangs up. I look at my next question

"You said in one of your speeches 'I am a rich man'"

"Is it not obvious?"

"Absolutely" before I read the next question, a caller is ready on the line

"Hello"

"Hello"

"Yes, you are live with give democracy a chance"

"My name is Bello Wahab from Minna"

"Your contribution please"

"As regards the statement IBB made as being a rich man which is obvious mostly to us that lives where he is from. My simple question is this, where would a retired army coup director and organizer have his money

from? He should tell us what jobs army officer does that earned him such a fortune, and he shouldn't be proud of the money he stole from me and you until he prove me wrong"

"Any respond to that as to where the money came from"

"Remember I was a president"

"You said you didn't take any Nigerian money"

"I kept them". I look into my questioning papers to continue the question

"...I will put clear water for all'...you said. '...electricity, telephone, education for all. I will put computer in every classroom, I will give every Nigerian a real phone not these money-burning gadget called cellular phones. All homes from Sokoto to Port Harcourt will be connected to the WWW'... is this still your promise"

"That is what I said and it is my promise"

"Hello, hello, hello" an impatient voice is on the phone

"Hello, you welcome to give democracy a chance"

"Thank you, I want to use..."

"Hello" I interrupt

"Hello, hello I am here"

"Good, would you like to tell us your name and where you calling from"

"Yes sure; I am Alhaji Garba Mumudu; State water corporation, Lafia- Nassarawa"

"Okay Alhaji Garba tell us your opinion"

"I am seeing all this promises of Mr Babangida as his usual game playing and fooling the Nigerians. He is going to break all these beautiful promises I bet. I just hope that, the Allah he mentioned will help him out from the scene. I know Allah will never allow his children to suffer continuously. I am happy he involved God in this election, thank you and God help Nigeria"

"About this beautiful promises"

"I am serious, I will keep my promises". The phone starts ringing again

"Hi" a young female voice answer as soon as I pick the ringing phone

"Hello, please tell us your name and where you calling from"

"I'm Ime Etteh from Port Harcourt" her sharp voice echoes from the speaker. Her ebullience startles me too

"Ime your voice sound so young, you want to tell us what you do for a living?"

"Yeah, I'm a final year political science student here in Uniport"

"Okay your view"

"It is very annoying hearing someone who had made mistakes and suppose to be in his penance therapy still bragging on a national TV, fooling and playing with a whole nation. He thinks he inherited every thing from his divinity. He said with conviction he will give water, electricity, telephone, education, computer, cell phone as if he has them all in his storeroom. He said we use money burning cellular phones but we have them now...this is a thing he never allowed in his regime because he feared it will stimulate and facilitate coup. Mr Babangida, everybody knows you can never provide

what you mentioned, if you can why couldn't Mr Babangida provide them in eight years as a solo administrator. Sorry Felix for your time, the last question and it will be directed to Mr Babangida..."

"Go ahead and you need not to be sorry, that is why we are here"

"Thank you, my question is this...what makes Mr Babangida thinks he can do all things as a share holder in the government what he couldn't do as a independent overseer?"

"Thank you Ime and let take the next call from Damboa- Borno"

"Hello"

"Hello"

"Hi" there is silence from the other end

"Helloooo"

"Hel…" the line cease after a piercing noise

"Sorry we lost that" I pick my papers and scrutinize the next question

"Your interview with the news paper 'This Day' on 6th September 2004, you talked about the Okibo report and also you slashed heavily on Retired Major General Ishola Williams...why?"

"You see Felix..."

"These are your words on his opinion that didn't favor your 07 dream, you said" I start quoting from my questioning papers

"...'as a matter of policy, I don't join issues with my juniors'...you claimed you started serving in the military before him and you retired as a four star general and he, as a two star" he is listening with intense curiosity

"Why all this rank issue coming up as a democrat"

"I don't join issues with my subordinates no matter how highly placed"

"A lot of people saw your reaction abstruse, just your old self. This is how one Anthony Akinola puts it... 'General Ibrahim Badamosi Babangida must be reveling in the controversy he continues to generate'...the speaker wonders what type of democratic leadership a potential IBB presidency will be in 2007. He is afraid of this kind of obsession of power..." he wants to say something but I'm still talking, he sneers and allow me to continue

"...this is your question Mr Babangida, you don't join issues with your subordinates, how would this work in a democracy"

"It will work"

"How"

"It worked before"

"You never had a demo..."

"Any difference?" he reply with a ridicule look and I decides to keep the topic for now

"In June 2004, you went to Ghana to join President J. A. Kufor in the 44th anniversary of their republican status"

"Yes I was invited"

"This is Ghana that was driven out from Nigeria years back, now the road map to West Africa"

"Ghana is doing really great"

"What will you link Ghana recent progress to"

"I think Rawlings did a great thing by taking out the old circling power people and that gave a way to new ideas and new generations"

"How did you see such moves in Nigeria"

"Well, honestly that will help Nigeria but I think that won't happens in near time"

"Rumor have it that ECOMOG operations were designed as a scheme to rescue your friend late Samuel Doe"

"He was my friend and as I have said earlier I honor friends"

"Let take this call. Abu Danka from Offa- Kwara hello"

"Hello"

"Before you proceed, can you tell what you are into Mr Danka"

"Thank you Felix. I'm the president of the Olive. This is an NGO that is dealing with initiatives of youth's empowerment. Basically, we are into how the youth will refocus themselves into building this nation. One of our targets is to educate the youth on not following the footsteps of these corrupt leaders. We are bringing programs upon the youth to fight the inevitable mental revolution in other to free them from these mental typology and social codification. It is obvious Mr Babangida is in breach of his legitimacy and the result is as the C18 British philosopher puts it... 'bad government violates the social contract which the ruler enjoys with the governed and this empowers the latter to rid themselves of the former'. Thank you and God help Nigeria"

"Thank you Abu and this is from Kontagora-Niger"

"Hello"

"Your name"

"Awa Ibrahim, a nurse"

"Your contribution"

"I had love to say this to Mr Babangida, can I use this chance to say hello to Mr Babangida?"

"Sure" Mr Babangida nods

"I had like to say that Mr Babangida should not see the public's expression as something against him but he should try to see it as their rights. When America got their independence from Britain in 1776, Thomas Jefferson drafting the independence declaration, said '…people's rights are life, liberty, pursuit of happiness etc, and the government is to secure these rights…that when ever any form of government becomes destructive of these ends. It is the right of the people to alter or abolish it'. The French revolution was self determination of sovereignty of a nation lay with its people therefore government is by the people and for the people. A government that cannot guarantee its people's needs should be change by the expression of the popular will. And this is what the Nigerian public is doing now. Thank you"

"Thanks nurse, I have the feeling you have wrong profession" she laughs

"Thanks Awa. Give democracy a chance, the number to call for your contributions- 881644372"

"Hello" another call

"Hello"

"You welcome to give democracy a chance"

"Thank you"

"Can you tell us your name and where you calling from"

"I am Akharale, professor of law in Harvard University law school"

"Good evening professor, nice having you with us"

"Thank you"

"Professor Akharale would like to contribute to this issue I guess"

"That is right" silence follow before he start to speak

"Your cross examination your honor" I add trying to put laughter on what is coming

"If however, there was or there is still anyone who still faintly harbor any doubt about the personal culpability of Mr Babangida in the grievous, prolonged and continue ruination of the Nigeria nation, such has now being dissipate, given the arrant self-glorification and illusion of grandeur. From all indications, the man is unrepentant, a sure measure of his limited intellectual acuity" he seize for a moment and the line crack before his voice come back

"Hello"

"Continue Prof."

"Good, here is a man who know how best to engage some of the good and credible intellectuals of Nigeria manpower to accomplish his devilish schemes. He is such a street being to spot good but hungry people with adequate cerebral power and initiates them to his term. But I tell you this, common sense and political decency should have tell IBB that he has forfeited his political locus steindi in the people's court, instead he is boasting to use letter bomb again, saying his group benefited from the June 12 annulment. This will show you the limit of his understanding of the tragedy he had caused. He still boasts of legacy. A legend needs no six million-naira security coverage to walk in the streets of Lagos for instance. If Mr Babangida doubts or cannot understand what I am saying let him

consult his lawyer or someone outside his circle for more explanation. God help Nigeria, thank you" the line stops.

"Still to come on the program more questions and phone calls after the short break don't go away. IBB live, in a moment.

"Welcome back" looking straight to the camera after the commercials and the producer signal me to read the next question

"On May 14th 2000, the Senate Committee Chairman on public account Mr Idris Abubakar confirmed to the nation through the Federal Radio Corporation of Nigeria in Kaduna that the Committee has instructed the governor of Central Bank of Nigeria to furnish his Committee with documents relating to your era, what were these documents"

"They were interested in documents on debt-buy back, the six billion of public fund they said was missing and other things"

"Then what happened, how did it go?"

"Nothing, nothing was done"

"Nothing was done in eight years, this is the voice of the people. Nothing was done in independent eight years leadership, what would be the magic in four years where power is divided, check and balance"

"I will do it"

"The Western societies are not too free with you"

"I am not too free with them too"

"You had a lot of ban on them in your regime"

"When these civic societies became a butt in my behind, I banned them. I have no apology for that. I will do the same when I become the president again in 2007"

"This reminds me of your words...'When you are for us, I am generous and grateful. When you are against us, I treat you like I treat enemy combatants. Those in doubt should ask Mamma Vatsa'...this sounds a murder confession and militarily horrifies democracy" Now phone calls are coming in like passengers in a rush hour Lagos traffic

"Hello" I manage to pick one of the calls that are jamming the central line

"H -e- l l o" a furious male voice pierce our ears

"Hello, please can you lower your TV set"

"Ok..." it takes few seconds

"...now can you hear me?" he ask after the whistling noise died down

"Yes! Better"

"Sorry about that"

"That's okay, would you like to tell us your name and where you calling from"

"I am Alhaji Ibrahim Shehu from Minna"

"Tell us your own side of the coin?"

"Really. I am speechless to hear a man who want to rule a democratic state speaks in such a military tone and idea, the message is nothing that he is coming back to continue his dictatorship and cruelty. I cry for Nigeria before hand, my heart weep and my mind sob for this country on the things that awaits it when IBB returns. I don't have a problem with Babangida as a person and I am convinced no one in this country does, my problem is he doesn't know who he is...bad...and he is convinced to continue with that badness. I will vote for him...but first he has to know that all he had done

in the past is of little or no good to the nation..." he seized and swallowed some liquid before he continue

"...he should accept the reality and that will be his first step to victory. Then he will dedicate himself to the nation voluntary and pass through normal moral orientation and convince the nation on this then he can contest to be the president, why not, he has right to it as a citizen, but a citizen must have the quality to be a president before he aspires, thank you and God help Nigeria"

"Than you Alhaji"

"That was from your home town, are you surprised people in you town don't support you"

"Not at all for I am equal to the task"

"Okay let get this from Damboa- Borno" a signal from the producer ask my to ask my questionnaire. I look through my questionnaire.

"What prompt you to signed Nigeria to the OIC?"

"I signed Nigeria to the OIC to show those who thought my commitment to Islam was a suspect"

"But that was too much and very unpatriotic to do, use a whole country to defend just what people say about you"

"Yes"

"So, for instance some people had accused you of being a coward, all you will do is to engage Nigeria in a war just to show them you are not"

"Anything can happen"

"You see why it very easy to agree with those who believe you can't run this country because you have not convince anybody democratically you can lead a better government"

"My dream is to rule and let my kids rule"

"Hello, Dupe from Lagos" I call out after pressing the hold button on the phone

"Hello" she chortle

"Your contribution"

"Thank you for the interesting issue and I hope this program will serve its purpose of making the Nigerians to rethink and decide their future and their children's' future. My contribution is that you need a quality to rule and that is what we are all asking Mr Babangida to show. If he claims he has one but till now we have not seen an iota of a quality that makes him a president" the phone stop and Babangida's face alienate. I try to see an easy question. I search my memory, there is no one and I pick my questionnaire on the table and flip through the pages, my searching eyes cut this one. Before I can read it, a call comes in

"Hello, hello, hel..." he rattles belligerently

"Hello we hear you"

"Yes I am Kadiri Usman a senate member from the second republic"

"Right Mr Usman"

"You see"

"Mr.."

"Sorry" he apologize realizing he had cut me off

"That is okay Mr Usman, just wanted to know if possible where you calling from"

"Oh sorry, I am here in Kotagora-Niger state"

"Okay"

"I was just going to say that Mr Babangida has taking this coming back to decoy people again and again. With no offence, if Mr Babangida had come for a come back, let say with an evidence that he is really changed. Let be sincere that in his military era, achievements was not convincingly roses. I wouldn't say it was all bad... It would be bias to say it was all or nothing at all. I make this point often that if Mr Babangida had put all his so called rich money into this country instead of hauling them to abroad that benefits him very little or nothing. Say he bought the NEPA and produces light for every one. Or buys the NITEL and make phone available to all even though we pay now to a private hand. That money every body says he stole would have been used for us. I tell you he would have been a hero at this coming back. Look for instance, despite Abiola ITT scandal but he employed thousands of people. If Babangida, say Babangida to mean every other money making politicians nowadays use their money to built private companies instead of buying home in Los Angels, or buying airplanes and taking money to white man accounts...you think the white man will stop you from bringing money to their account...forget it. We should work for history and not name because our history is going to give us name". Mr Usman stops to catch his breathe. I don't want to interrupt. I'm hoping for more and Mr Babangida is just too bore listening to this Mr Know it all and he had been in the government but didn't do anything for the country.

Just run your mouth and keep quite he might have murmured to himself.
He careless of his sententious blabbing

"You see..." Mr Usman continues. I have no intension to shorten his
time, I want to hear more and I'm convinced the viewers are enjoying to
hear them-them firing at each other

"Say Mr Babangida had involved in the country's bureaucracy...like
serve as an ambassador or represented Nigeria nationally or internationally,
people had monitored his works and he, gaining confidence of the people, I
mean we all should learn from our mistakes"

"Thank you Mr Usman. I turn to my guest"

"You said in your 2007 presidential candidate acceptance speech, your
words '...I will send out men and women and ask them to go there and
conquer the world. The men shall reach every nook and cranny of the globe
by mails. The women will find their way to the streets of Italy, Frankfurt,
London and Moscow'..." I stop reading from my questionnaire as a ringing
phone persist

"Hello you welcome to give democracy a chance"

"Thank you. First I will like to say compliments for the program"

"Thank you"

"I am calling form Benin City and my name is Abigel"

"Okay Abigel here you are lets hear your voice"

"Well, I am 37 years old and I have been away from Nigeria since I
was 19. It was Babangida regime that forced me out of this country. I know
what it is to nook and crack in a land you will be treated as a foreigner.
When you nook in foreign land, I mean nook not nooky, then you will

understand what I'm talking about. I know what it is and I have seen it for a women to find her way to the streets of Italy and..." her voice deepen and you can tell she is coming to cry. She blows her nose and continues

"...and I can assure you that to be a Nigerian girl in the streets of Italy is not an enviable experience" her crying tone concludes.

"Ok..."

"There is a question I had like to ask Mr Babangida"

"Go ahead Abigel"

"I want to know if Mr Babangida really will send his citizens abroad to duplicates bank cards and swallows drugs in other to get it to the dying consumers and send his girls to the streets of Italy"

"Thank you Abigel, I respect your feelings and I can understand your mood. It's nice you express it. This is the fruit of democracy...one can express his feelings and the other can agree or disagree with him or her. So this brings us to the next question but not till our guest express myself on this last caller's comment, if not we will be moving to the next question" his feeling is obvious he is not ready to comment and I have to help him skip through

"Right..." I look at my questioning papers to read another line

"In a very popular American web site, it is boldly written that the American government and many other western governments says your rule for long eight years has absolutely nothing to show for it, except more of the same..." his eyes widen and his mouth moves but refuse to say a word

"...when you come back, don't you think you might have difficulty in creating good relationship with this countries since they don't believe in you and you have not show any improvement since you left office"

"No problem at all. I will do it"

"How?"

"Trust me"

"How will you expect my trust when I can't see no evidence. The trust will be hard to give, especially when I have been a victim before"

"Hello" I answer another call

"Hello"

"You are live with give democracy a chance"

"My name is Gabriel Uduka, professor in philosophy at Ilorin.

I choose this simple logic as a premise to explain my mind to Mr Babangida"

Okay, let hear it prof."

"I was hungry one day, very, very hungry and Mr Babangida walked in. A handsome man, the finest I have seen, dressed with a lace materials... don't cry he said. I am going to Lagos, when I come back I will bring you food. Oh thank you baba I said and waited. At dark hour, the hunger was at my throat, here he comes... oh boy he said I didn't have money to buy your food..." he stops for a second and we all waits for continuation

"Hello..."

"Yes we're here go ahead"

"Okay I slept with hunger. A week later here comes the man, handsome than before...oh you hungry, don't worry, I will buy you food from Abuja... and I said you got money to buy the food, he said don't worry. I need to get more worried Felix"

"No doubt I can feel you"

"Mr Babangida has failed us, if he wants to lead again he need to show us how, thank you for giving me this space"

"The space is yours and thank you for your beautiful analogy" I turn to my guest

"A document prepared by scientology guided by Chief E. Okafor in June 2000 talking about 'senate committee on public accounts' said Nigerian leaders have stolen or misappropriated State funds estimated N400 billions about 40 billion US dollars and your regime stands the highest frauded government ever"

"I don't know what is scientology or who is that Okafor"

'Referring to you, A Chicago based Nigerian Mr Okpara...'a Nigeria fox can not be trusted to guard a Nigerian hen house"

"He is an Igbo, let him come here to say that"

"In your regime, there are so many public funds that have never be accounted for till day"

"That is not true"

"Minton said he would testify before the Nigeria Senate if summoned on the pay-back deal"

"Nobody is going to call him"

"A statement issued by the office of president Obasanjo said no investigation in your affairs because there is no evidence against you. '...the government can not launch a blind probe' he said". This time the victorious smile in his face reveals the space between his teeth.

"But a former Nigeria bishop Bolande Gbonigethe said no prosecution because Obasanjo is your business partner"

"Point of correction…" he starts with abuzz irritation

"Obasanjo is not my business partner, I invested on him"

"Professor Omo Omoruyi…" a timid smile craw to his lips as I mention the name

"You know him right?"

"He is my man"

"About June 12, this is what he said '…the June 12 was the day IBB in concert with his colleagues then commenced the act of gross denial of the right to human dignity of the Nigerian people; the act of betrayal of the democratic rights of Nigeria. This is a fervent appeal to a friend who I know even though he would not say so openly had been tormented by the development since the annulment and arrest and eventual death of chief Abiola. May I in friendship and humility and because of many years of our close personal respect in the past, counsel you to feel sorry for what you did… and you should know that it is for your unwillingness to apologize to the Nigeria people is responsible for president Obasanjo's inability to do something about contemplation how to immortalize anything about June 12… and your action would free Obasanjo from obvious constraints.

"Poor president, a real puppet"

"He listens when I talks"

"Professor Omoruyi wise words sound like a real friend's words"

"I don't need these kind of words". I look through my questionnaire and find a short question

"People describes Abacha as your" I look at the note to read the word

"…henchman"

"He was. Yeah…" hesitates as he huffs into a deep memories

"Hello" another call

"Hello"

"Yes you welcome to give democracy a chance"

"Thank you"

"Would you like to tell us your name and where you are calling from"

"Usman Jaji, member; National population commission"

"Right Mr Jaji"

"Ability dependent entirely upon a greater and better understanding…"
Jaji starts with a premise

"…Understanding of that field or office in which one cares to be more able. If Mr Babangida agrees with me on this concept which I hope he would, then he need to see with me why he can not lead this country now till he have shown better understanding of governing well. An essential factor he have not shown to the nation"

"Thanks Mr Jaji for your contribution"

"No thanks I am doing what I ought to do as a belonger to this country"

"Mr Babangida?" I try to have him respond but the willingness was slow. I'm scrutinizing my next question from the questioning papers when the phone starts to ring

"Hello and you are live with give democracy a chance"

"Hello I am Alhaji Musa Bakuomi, a business man from Gusau-Zamfara"

"Your contribution Jubril"

"*Thanks Felix and hi everybody. I personally respect and admire Mr Babangida for his single mindedness in his course. The fact is Mr Babangida do not have or have not shown the characteristic of a democratic leader. A good leader need to respect restrictions; the restrictions of a government gives the sovereign-the citizens their freedom. Without respected restrictions, the citizens are slave, doomed to fear of uncertainty in all actions around them. I am afraid Mr Babangida lacks the spirit to accept restrictions. Thank you and God help Nigeria*"

"*Thanks Alhaji*" *I decide to bring down Mr Babangida tension with a simple question but a call is ready*

"*Hello*'

"*Hello*"

"*Yes, you are live in give democracy a chance*"

"*Thank you*"

"*Please your name*"

"*Garuba Umar Dutse, Jigawa*"

"*What is your profession Mr Umar*"

"*A senate in the second republic*"

"*Right, you will like to contribute to this issue*"

"*Sure*"

"*Okay, go ahead*"

"*You see, I pity Nigerians so much now that we forget history so soon. I am surprised that some body with clear eyes will come out openly to say IBB should rule again. This is a man that lives by killing, evidence upon evidence of all he had killed just to rule us the way he wants. I want to tell these hungry, cheap, ignorant followers that sell their future and their children's future by going to Minna at the weekend to collect their payment. This is a man we should ask how Bola Igie was killed just few days to his 79th birthday. This dutiful patriot was cut off just to have PDP vote in south-south" he swallows some saliva and continues*

"This is a man who put a bomb inside the airplane that killed high ranked officers. All these still hang on his neck, instead of advocating for his trial, you collect money and say come back. Come back to do what, even you; the supporters, you will not escape from the hand of the merciless IBB and because you aid him in his trading act. You will share from the nemesis".

"Okay..." I try to cut him off

"I am through Felix and God help Nigeria"

"Amen O" I look into my questionnaire

"And Obasanjo is not really your friend"

"He is my friend, I gave him money"

"It sound you gave him money to buy his freedom"

"Does it?"

"All these are coming out when you are not in power, what about when you comes in, what will happen?"

"I will continue to do what I have being doing"

"In 2002, Newswatch sought Gani Fawehinmi opinion on the far reaching recommendations of the Human Rights Violations Investigation commission in the allegation that you murdered journalist Dele Giwa and Abiola. There is a link of this man...General Abdulsami Abubakar?"

"I don't want to drag my cousin into any thing" I respect this and I won't go further because Abubarkar deserve a great respect. I will meet with him one day and tell him I respect his service to the nation. He is my most fanciful Nigeria general

"Fawehinmi confirmed this in record...'you (General Ibrahim Badamosi Babangida met with Obasanjo shortly after he was released from prison. And you proposed to Obasanjo to become the president" I read the last line on a center page in my questioning file now resting on my laps. I flip the page and start to read from the upper line in the following page

"The story continued that Obasanjo told you that Abiola was still alive though he was in the prison. Then you told him, reassuring him every thing would be taken care of at any rate. In fact you did took care of things and Abiola did mysteriously died shortly after your meeting with Obasanjo" his look betrays the hidden acerbity. What's this, a confession for murder? Well crime investigators should know better

"In your 2007 presidential candidate acceptance speech you confirmed you killed Dele Giwa?"

"What! No I didn't"

"You said quote...'if we have to use letter bomb again, you bet that we will'"

"I said we would use letter bomb again if the needs arise"

"Where else have you used letter bomb Mr Babangida? If you have to use it again that means you have use it before right?"

"I can't answer that right now"

"Fawehinmi said you should be arrested with no further delay and place in custody, arranged before a court of law and prosecuted by the ministry of Justice. If you are found guilty, you should face the music and be executed by the normal ordinary process of hanging as stipulated under the law of Nigeria...that is the only way General Ibrahim Badamosi Babangida would be seen not to be above the laws of Nigeria'"

"Well..." he wants to say something but let it go

"Mr Babangida, don't you think this record on your meeting with Obasanjo need to be investigated?"

"Who is going to investigate? No body will do that"

"There are laws that guides us in this country and in this case, there are rules of law to follow"

"Who made those laws, law can not make itself"

"Statistics have it that Obasanjo failed in his two terms government because you are always there in a threatening shadow telling him, what are you doing, common do it this way or do it that way"

"When you send somebody market, the person should buy what you ordered for and not what comes into his head on his way"

"What is this referring to?"

"I spoke in parables, try to analyze the meaning"

"Obasanjo is acting with fear"

"No, no he is respecting the rules of the game"

"But I have a right to see his attitude as coward"

"What will he do?..." a call comes in

"Hello"

"Hi Felix, bravo for your program"

"Thank you, you would like to contribute on the topic right?"

"Yes please"

"Okay go ahead but not before you tell us and the viewers your name and where you calling from; if you want to anyway"

"Sure, I am Obukogho from Asaba, Delta State"

"Good". An irritating noise whistle from the TV screen that monitor the live broadcast

"Can you reduce the volume of your TV?"

"It is reduced already"...the noise decrease

"Okay continue"

"I want to comment on your last question of whether Obasanjo is acting with fear, the answer is obviously yes. It's most disappointing for Obasanjo to become a puppet before his junior officer. He, Obasanjo should take example from the governor of Anambra State: Ngige who the Okija lords helped to the office and tried to dictates his affairs but he refused to be a puppet and set them up. Let me make myself clear, I don't side the governor in the first place been part of evil at all, because you can't use evil to fight evil but it works to some point. Now, though the Okija lords exist, they had lost their mafiaism in Anambra polities. Lastly, I would say and advice Obasanjo to get his butt together and probe Mr Babangida"

"Well viewers" I manage to say as my face show on the monitoring screen

"Before we take more calls, let have some words from Mr Babangida and many more calls but before that let have some commercials, give democracy *a chance live when we come back, don't go away" the camera show the tired look on Mr Babangida's face but he has be doing well hiding it for over an hour now. Soon the show resume*

"Obasanjo obviously lack the capacity to say you should be investigated"

"I don't know, all I know is I shouldn't be investigated"

"But then he is risking being examine for culpability when he leaves office"

"When I come back to my office, I will do anything I feel is right to be done. If Obasanjo bears culpability for whatever reason, he will surely be examined"

"You didn't go to court to stop Justice Oputa from submitting the HRVIC report"

"No I didn't"

"How on earth did you get all these information?"

"I need nobody to knock the door of the president for me, I need no one to ask question or information for me. I live among my people"

"Chief Gani Fawehinmi said Obasanjo is guilty of this"

"They should settle that themselves"

"When the honorable member of the Federal House of Representatives from Zamfara State was recently jailed in Saudi Arabia for allegedly importing fake US dollar bills into the Arab country and trying to bribe the Saudi Authority to release his uncle in jail there for unknown crime... this is how a foreign reporter puts it '...as if to add transgression to grievance (possession of fake dollar bills) the Zamfara 'Honorable'"... honorable in

bracket '...even tried to bribe the authorities in Saudi Arabia in other to secure the release of his uncle, they way he would have done very effortlessly in Nigeria..." he wants me to heat the nail at the head, his look urging for the question if there was any

"...he would have done effortlessly in Nigeria, that qualifies us, Nigeria as something?"

"This people don't know how to handle things, that is why I must go there"

"Nigerians, I mean Nigerian officers abuse their diplomatic passports, that's horrendous"

"Well..." a phone call cut him off

"Hello, hello, hello" the impatience masculine voice begin to echo through the phone speakers ready to starts argument

"Yeah hello, you are welcome to the program"

"Please Felix allow me to comments on this issue you just raised in your question about the abuse of diplomatic passport. I happened to work with the Nigerian embassy in four European countries and two countries in South America. I will sadly say that not only we practice exactly the negativities we practice here in Nigeria over there but about 20,000 Nigerian diplomatic passports are currently in circulation. More sadly, the high office men and women issue diplomatic passports to their children, boyfriends, girlfriends which they then abuse for their personal holidays, health care trips, business transactions, financial maneuvers and general escapism, this is UN observation and the boom started in Babangida regime. You see these vacuous and pillaging leaders..."

"Right..." I cut him short and turn to my guest

"How are you reacting to this" He drags the edge to his agbada to his shoulders. The calling number shows beneath the TV screen.

"In my period, I only gave diplomatic passport to those I trusted"

"Diplomatic passports are not for you, they belong to the government. You don't give it to those you want to..."

"I have said it before, then I was in change"

"Are all these going to repeat itself when you come in in 2007?"

"I believe what I did when I was in office was a good thing. If I come back more likely, as a matter of fact it is going to repeat itself"

"Hello, you are live with us on give democracy a chance" I answer another call

"Hi Felix, I am Godfrey Uteh from Uyo"

"Go ahead Godfrey"

"Just a little comment on Mr Babangida..."

"Mr Babangida is listening" everyone laughs except Babangida himself who welcomed the joke with a grin

"Please Godfrey continue"

"Ok...I think Mr Babangida issue right now is he can not draw a line between freedom and barriers. And he failed and keeps failing to realize that when the relationship between freedom and barriers become too imbalanced, the end result is unhappiness. The truth is, a man who is willing to accept restrictions and barriers and he is not afraid of failure is free but a man who fight restrictions and barriers will usually, more likely to be trapped"

"Thank you, thank you very much Godfrey for that and would Mr Babangida like to say something on this" he shows intension of responding. His body language...

"You declared in a Jos Seminar that you didn't rule Nigeria but you reengineered it?"

"That's right"

"As an engineer, has your construction project passed for commission?"

"No commission yet?"

"A contract you signed, not yet commission after about how is it?" I make a quick calculation

"21years?"

"You know things are slow in Nigeria"

"Coming back to probing your administration the then governor of Central Bank of Nigeria; Abulkadir Ahmed who could have put more light on your squandering, especially on the Gulf war oil windfall is dead"

"Even if he was alive, it wouldn't have made any difference"

In an article revelation from Tell magazine on your power game titled 'IBB's NEW GAMEPLAN', you wanted to snatched the presidency from Obasanjo in 2003"

"Yes"

"What happened?"

"I looked at the situation and I realized it wasn't time to take my office back"

"How did you realize that?"

"Well, some ...oh many northerners shifted their support to Alex Ekwueme or Chief Emeka, Anyaolu. I tried the east but Joe Nwodo or Ogbonnya Onu was gaining ground. I tried to walk with Sunday Awoniyi who was a kind of known amongst his people to have him work on Obasanjo in the south but..." he stop to reflect as if he is trying to adjust what went wrong then. The silence persist and I tries to bring him back to the studio

"But..." I encourage like a psychologist advancing in an emotional distress therapy case

"I found out it wasn't going to be easy, so I decides to have patience and turned myself in"

"And now here you are"

"Here I am"

"Okay, let come back to this before we take our next call. In your State creation, visible corruption erupted..."

His nervousness is rising up. His trademark smile vanished almost an hour ago

"...will you tell the nation why Asaba was made the capital city of Delta State?"

"It is simple. I was a soldier, I didn't know anything about geography or anything about landscape or demography but what I do know is my wife is from Asaba and I made Asaba the Delta State capital base on that"

"And what about Anioma. Any good reason why Anioma was unsolicitedly moved from old Benin province to the old Delta?"

"I can't found any better reason now than the one written on a paper for me to read but I think...oh I remember now that I am talking about it.

The reason was that Anioma will proliferates in Delta more rapidly than the way it would in its stagnant position in the old Benin..."

"Just a moment of interruption Mr Babangida for the commercial break and you will continue" I face the camera

"Viewers you watching give democracy a chance with us today is Mr Babangida, a retired Nigerian army General and one time military head of state and now PDP presidential candidate for 2007 election. More questions and phone calls to take don't go away. IBB live on give democracy a chance, when we come back" the monitoring TV switched to a running projector and a mobile phone company shows it's latest free minutes offer. The commercial lasted 45 seconds and my face return on the monitoring screen on the producer's table

"Welcome back" but the phone is already ringing

"I suggest we take the call before you answer all together,

"Hello"

"Hello Mr Felix"

"Hello caller, Felix is okay by me but I respect your formality if that is what you prefer but I am more comfortable with Felix. Anyhow go ahead and make your contribution"

"Thanks and compliments for your simplicity"

"I am not paying you for this advert". I laugh with him and other back stage crew except Babangida

"Go ahead caller"

"Okay, I want to quickly say that it is human for Mr Babangida to do what he has done but if I were him, very happy I am not, I had sit down

and be going through a moral rehabilitation rather than seeking office of his incapability. It is most bizarre and bad for a ruler to historically ignore Warri as the capital and choose Asaba just because his wife is from there..."

"Okay..."

"...and lastly it is very rude, greed, unqualified of him as he has shown no indifference to the action, seeking back the office you made mess out of is equal to verbally insulting about 150 million nation's population"

"Okay..."

Thank you and God help Nigeria"

"Before you go would you like to tell us your name and where you calling from?"

"Sure, I am Thomson Ogherobo from Warri"

"Thank you Thomson for your view. Now this brings us to the next question..." he reset himself and flaps his tailored brocade to his shoulder.

"Recently you were the president's emissary to Sudan?"

"Yes. I wanted to be there"

"People including me marvels on how you are able to seize the central stage in Nigeria political arena"

"I learned the game" his confidence is returning and the fatigue on his face giving way to the trade mark smile. The sparkling teeth starts showing. This interview had made me to know him better. The reason why IBB became the most discussed president in recent times began to form in my reasoning. It's not because he is a bad leader, it wasn't because he was the worst military ruler- a symbol of all that is most decoy, abstruse and *his acuity maneuvering, no he adore himself with the anthem of the most virulent face of the autocracy. For this reasons I am convinced the people's preponderant cry for help should be more audible. Except the help come soonest, Babangida's acuity abash in his natural self with such an overarching ambition power by dubious wealth that he continue to see himself as the Nigeria constitution.*

"Mr Babangida, can we talk about your educational background?"

"Why not" he reply with a frustrating tone but with a relax mind. I open my questionnaire to the center page. I begin to read from the top line in the left page

"You are amongst Nigerian children of the early forties"

"Yes I was born in 19941"

"And you started primary school nine years after your birth"

"Yes in 1950"

"Then you attended secondary school"

"Yes, government college Bida"

"No evidence you had a secondary school certificate"

"Go to the school and ask, it is a long time now"

"Anyhow, you were twenty one when you entered the army"

"December 10, 1962"

"Two years later you were in India military camp to learn how to handle secret information"

"Yes for few months"

"Another two years passed before you were in UK for three months to lean how to drive armor cars"

"Yes that was 1966"

"And in 1970 you went back to UK for another three weeks on a commander's seminar" he shakes his head for the answer and start getting uneasy with the accuracy of the information

"You leant more on Armory in The United States for six months in the fall of 1972 and when you came back mid 1973, you were giving the post of Lieutenant-Colonel"

"The post eventually came to me in 1974"

"Very big office to obtain with six months camping and three weeks seminars"

"They gave it to me"

"And another six months camping at the Command and Staff College, Jaji won you the rank of a Brigadier"

"That is correct"

"And to get the rank of 'Star' you were in Jos for strategic studies and again the normal six month training but this time in international defense management course in the US"

"Then I became Major General"

"Lastly in 1987 you needed no day camping or a week seminar to attain the highest army rank...as head of State you gave yourself the rank of full STAR General"

"At last"

"Now, looking at your educational resume', people would say you have a very low or insufficient academic capacity that is a priority I mean a prerequisite to fit into a modern democratic polities"

"*Well...*"

"*And just in a second if you may allow my interruption*" *the politeness left him no choice. He nod reluctantly*

"*...and to rise to a full star general, three weeks, six month training, would that guarantee your professional capability and ability as a full star general in bracket?*"

"*I had always acted as a General*"

"*Could your low educational background have contributed to your failure in government?*"

"*I didn't fail and I studied*"

"*In Indian camps or British military seminars on how to drive military van*"

"*In Jos*"

"*Still on military. We are on human relations, diplomacy and not on war fare*"

"*It is normal here, Obasanjo, Abacha what did they have that qualified them, nothing*"

"*Hello*" *a call*

"*Hello*"

"*Hello*"

"*Yes go ahead*"

"*Hello*"

"*I can hear you...*"

"*Hello...*" *the line faint and busy tone come up. This time my mind has soften for my guest, I begin to see the real him not this political IBB but IBB of a person. He is normal, not a monster-a gentle, emotional human whose ideology supersede his HIM. I wished reverse could be the case, the ringing phone awake me from my daydreaming*

"Hello"

"Hello"

"Hello go ahead"

"Hello every body, my name is Fred Agiobiagbe from Shagamu"

"Go ahead Fred"

"I just want to comment on the last issue which is the educational incapability a lot of our leaders lacks. We can see why they failed, we are conscious of that, we don't want that to happen again. We have paid enough price for our leaders' incapability, enough, we need a change and Mr Babangida should play the role of a leader who will lead to select good people. He knows these good men and women here in Nigeria. Instead of corrupting them to his trade, choose them, protect them and let them work with their real hearts and abilities...work for the nation and not for you. He should help us for that change in other to have his heroism in the memory of this nation. Thank you and God help Nigeria"

"Thank you Fred"

"How is our future Mr Babangida, it seems Nigerians are giving you more specific role to play in Nigeria polities. They want you to be a director and watcher rather than a player"

"The future is going to come definitely"

"Don't this role gives you a kind of obligation to work with the people rather than to work against them"

Felix O. Vescovi

"I will walk with my people"

"If they say you will work better for them in point A and you say no I am in point B, won' this bring conflicts"

"Conflicts will be resolved"

"The whole nation follow your order?" the phone start to ring

"Hello, hello..."

"Hello"

"Good evening to everybody in the studio and the viewers at home"

"Good evening and you are welcome to the program give democracy a chance"

"Thank you"

"Would you like to tell us your name, where you calling from and your contribution"

"Sure, my name is Tude Olatubosun from Abeokuta"

"Okay your contribution"

"First I will like to thank the organizer and producer of this program for telling us more of IBB. My case is very simple and it is this looking back at Mr Babangida and his regime I feel skeptical when he comes out to say he will bring a good government back in 2007. He have since concern himself only in promoting his name and not convincing us on how he will actually rule us good, all his talks and conferences never show or try to convince the nation of his good intension but succeeded in showing how he will repeat his old self and this perhaps pose a direct question to Mr Babangida... how are you going to cope with the democratic tussles of power balance and sharing, disagreements, dialogues which you are not used to..."

" *I must say this…*" *his tone is warming up and his molested dignity surfacing*

"Okay Tude" I intercept and turn to my gust

"Has Tude's analysis show reasons why you IBB is not qualify to rule Nigeria…?"

"But I must rule now"

"You said all things should be for the interest of the nation and its' people"

"Absolutely"

"If your ruling again is a thing of MUST, don't you see you contradict your statement… doing things for the interest of the nation and its' people and you shifting the whole idea of doing things in the interest of the nation into a greed…" I look into his direction, he is looking at me but he is not listening. He is far way…melancholy and a distracted dreamer.

"A lot of critics claim your book's title… ' A heritage of Reform' is inappropriate"

"That is the title I chose for the book"

"Many Northerners are not really for you"

"How?"

"I mean they are against you…like the 2002 demonstration in Kano where people were shouting publicly in a humiliating chorus 'Sai Buhari, Sai Buhari'…what is the meaning of that?"

"Ask them, you can call one of the demonstrators for interview"

"That is an idea, isn't it?" he is thinking if he has not undone himself with the suggestion

"Never mind"

" Haiya Tombai, your coordinator in 2003"

"Yes?"

"He said you are your wife personal property"

"I don't know how he came to know that. He was to coordinate my 2003 vision and not my family, so what ever he says is irrelevant and he should go and face his own wife that is..." he cease, a big word was to come out of his mouth. He realizes the gravity of the word and shakes his head in ostentation

"In your Jos book launch, you said you re-engineered Nigeria"

"Yes I did"

"Where is Olu Falae, the SAP designer?"

"He is somewhere in the south making mouth with no money. Nobody is listening to him" a smile curve out from his lips

"Who is Abubakar and why did you trust him so much?"

"He is my brother..." he stops for a moment before he continues. He gazes at the ceiling as if to get his divinity attention to remind him of what he will say about Abubakar

"...he is my adopted brother. His father brought me up, I went to be with them when I was a baby and since I am a year older than him, we grew up as a senior brother and junior brother"

"Your natural parents?"

"Yes?"

"They were Muhamend and Aisha Babangida?"

"Yes"

"Is it to clear that sense of orphanage, that you gave your parents names to your 'heirship'" he is quiet and a phone call interrupts the silence

"Hello"

"Hello, I am Olu Omogbemi from Ikerre-Ekiti"

"Okay, you contribution"

"I want to clear this from Mr Babangida, it is obvious he is not willing to comment on his birth background. I want to say that Mr Babangida, have no reason to be avoiding his childhood. It was not your making. You didn't choose it yourself. I am an orphan, Bill Clinton; former US president is an adopted child. As a matter of fact, that is why you should be proud and be a role model to the poor and unprivileged That is why may be God has brought you up from grass to grace to be there for the poor. I am using this opportunity to remind you of your mission Mr Babangida that good life is not about names, money, and titles but about how much you influence people positively. We poor, we unprivileged, we helpless, we are looking forward to you. We need you cos you have been there. You know what it is to be poor, fatherless and that is why you must come back to your mission as a role model to the poor" he is about crying

"Please Mr Babangida, look at the suffering of your people and forget about your accounts and your houses and names and your name will last longest in the memory of your people, thank you and God help Nigeria". When the phone cease, the sensitivity of the call keeps me blushing and I wish Mr Babangida feel that way. Maybe.

"What a word" I manage to say hoping Babangida could feel the way I was feeling. I pray instantly the words touch him the way they have touched me.

"These are hard words to consume Mr Babangida"

"Sort of"

"Your adopted brother Abubakar is very quiet"

"That is his nature"

"He is one of the few Generals who never really hold a political office"

"That is true, he wanted to serve his country more than holding posts"

"He was the master of ceremony, that saluting solder on a horse in presidential swearing in ceremo…"

"Yes when Obasanjo gave power to Shagari"

"What a rotation in 1999 when he was to give power to Obasanjo" he smiles

"He is married to a high court Judge?"

"Yes a very brilliant woman …Fatima"

"Why is it that we can't even hear Abubakar's name in all this political noise, and he is the last General from the arena"

"As I said, he is a quiet man, he doesn't like confusion"

"Why did he become head of State, you need to like confusion to be a head of state"

"He never wanted to, he hate being there. I had forced him to do it for me"

"For you?"

"Yes, I needed to come back and after Abacha turned out the way he did, I never saw anybody closer I could use than him"

"He agreed?"

"He had no choice but you can see how he willingly left the power"

"Yes, in eleven months that was unusual for a Nigeria military"

"He is an usual man"

"Where is him now as a retired soldier"

"He is sick"

"Sick?"

"Yes with a neurological seizures"

"Oh!" my heart feel for a man of such quality and I pray silently for his recovering and I don't know if I can put myself up again to ask any further question about him, at least not for now

"I like to see him in the Nigeria reconstruction, after the propose constitutional investigation anyway"

"He is sometimes working with the UN"

"Really"

"Yes"

"I wish him well"

"Thank you"

"In 1995, Lawan Gwadabe and his mates attempted a coup"

"Yes"

"This March 1st, how do you remember it"

"Obasanjo and Yar'Adua helped him to plan the coup"

"What happened?"

"I watched them"

"Okay, when Abacha your friend hanged Saro-Wiwa despite the appeals for mercy. I say mercy that is a wrong word to use because he was saying the truth. Anyhow, mercy from all international bodies... where were you?"

"We were not all that close at this time, I was busy working on him"

"At last you succeeded"

"Obviously"

"But then, Nigeria suffered all that followed like our suspension from the commonwealth and Mandela calling for international sanctions against Nigeria oil"

"I am not responsible for that"

"Oladipo Diya tried another coup again December 21 1997"

"I think it was a set up..."

"This is speculation"

"Right I was not there, but I am convinced it was a set up for Diya who was growing strong for Abacha at that period"

"But no coup succeeded in Abacha's period"

"Abacha was a strong man. He had be with me in all coups, he knew the dos and the don'ts in coup and no coup would have removed him"

"That is why you use other method?" his respond comes slowly with abash smile. It's not the convincing trademark smile. It's a sinister reaction of un-regrettable moment.

"Abacha was your close person"

"Yes we were tag team"

"Then what happened"

"Nothing really till when I heard in April 1998 that he was now the only nominated candidate for the presidency. My blood rippled in my veins"

"How were you able to use Ernest Shonekan. He listened and did what you expected him to do. He didn't divert from your instructions"

"No he didn't"

"How were you able to do that to a well read man as he is"

"When I left, I gave instructions to Abacha but the real person that was doing the watching was my boy Aliyu Mohammed Gusau who I left with Shonekan as still the National Security Adviser"

"But why this British oriented Shonekan?"

"Shonekan was long studied. His original role was that of Augustus Aikhomu. He was to be my vice President when I will become a full civilian president. But when the June 12 issue disorganized my plans, I was left with no option than to let him in"

"When he came in that 1993, he never knew he was going to spend 82 days in the office"

"Well I explained the situation to him before he came"

"But not he was to spend some days as president"

"No"

"So you were forced by pressure to leave office"

"That is correct"

"In your VOA Hausa service interview, this controversial only God can Stop you from being the president come 2007..."

"Look..."

"...*your words were what God has ordain...*" *I read from my questionnaire*

"*That is it*"

"*It seems you forget history so soon. Don't you think history can repeat itself?*"

"*How?*"

"*That the same pressure that forced you out in 1993 can still force you not to be president comes 2007*" *His face darken and his reasoning agitating as if he have just thought about this for the first time. The veins on his forehead become more visible.*

"*How did you use Shonekan to setup Abiola before the members of the diplomatic corps in Nigeria*"

"*It wasn't easy, I issued fraudulent payment vouchers to Shonekan to show to the corps as evidence of an attempt by Abiola to compromise the integrity of the chairman of electoral commission*"

"*And he indeed carried out what you told him*"

"*Yes*"

"*Shonekan resigned as head of state after 82 days and 83 nights*"

"*Yes*"

"*Why?*"

"*I don't want to say much on this because Abacha, Diya, Gwadabe surprised me*"

"*And you tried to surprise them especially Abacha the head*"

"*Yes*"

"You tried to surprise Abacha in 1997 using Obasanjo, Yar'Adua, and the same Lawan Gwadabe"

"Yes but Abacha's North Korean trainers"

"North Korea?"

"His security advisers were North Korean Military"

"Wow"

"And he also had a secret service operations from Libya"

"So the whole coup flopped"

"Yes"

"You were not touched"

"No body mentioned my name"

"Why are you so influential?"

"Because I was the only member in the MSC that serve on all military councils since 1975"

"But Shonekan claimed his abdication to Abacha was voluntary"

"Look Shonekan claim anything you tell him to claim"

"So it was never voluntary as he claimed"

"It was not a voluntary submission. I have never seen a voluntary submission of power except Abubakar, even that of Dr. Nwafor Orizu to J. Agwuiyi-Ironsi in 1966 was not voluntary"

"The death of Ikoku, Yar'Adua, Abacha, Abiola and his wife. The eventful coronation of Obasanjo they are all mysterious"

"Try to ask lawyer Oladipo Diya (Esq.), he will tell you more on all this"

"In your regime, siphoning of national treasury was at its peak and continues with such gravity till now"

"In my period I fought against all corruption and..." the phone is ringing now

"Hello"

"Hi Felix"

"Hi there"

"I am Saratu from Potsikum- Yobe"

"Your contribution"

"I just want to point blank...tell Mr Babangida that he was responsible for the siphoning of Nigeria treasure that characterize his regime because he legalized national loathing into Nigeria tradition and mentality that now stands a cancer to us"

"Thank you Saratu and Mr Babangida have a chance to say something on this"

"As I have said, my period was clean"

"In one of your speeches, you made mentioned of your intelligent, elegant Children especially the dude sons Mohammed and Aminu. You said they have grow up into fine gentlemen...' it is my hope you added '...that one day like the Bushes, my sons will serve this nation of ours'...you have prepared their political hereditary?"

"You know I will never tell you yes or no but I will tell you this that God will determine their political ambitions"

"Your wife Hayija Maryam King-Babangida is seen by many as the Hillary Rodham-Clinton of Nigeria"

"Is she?"

"In 1989 she won the woman of the year by the New Nigeria. She was awarded the international recognition Award by the Harlem Women Committee of the USA"

"Yes"

"The chairman of the national economic intelligence Committee (NEIC) professor Ibrahim Ayagi accused you publicly of destroying the nation's economy"

"He should come and say that to me face to face"

"Now let take this call from Zamfara, hello" busy tone beeps when I press the hold button on the phone set.

"We lost that" another call comes

"Hello" I answer a call

"Hello, I am Uduak Etokebe from Uyo"

"Go ahead Uduak"

"I want to comment on professor Agayi's accuse, can we the nation ignore such a serious accusation from such an expert and vote Mr Babangida in again when has not shown any sign different from his old self. What he always thinks is Nigeria is a banana republic or Babangida island. He ought to be a role model for the poor, the weak and his role is not to rule now but to stay clear from polities. Thank you and God help Nigeria"

"Thank you over there in Akwa-Ibom" I look through my questionnaire

"*A panel audit headed by a respectable economist Dr. Pius Okigbo confirmed that fund running into 12.4 billion dollar including the Gulf war windfall were misappropriated by your regime between 1985-1993*"

"*That Okigbo report is fake*"

"*What about John Fashenu issue. He said his three years investigation that cut several non-Nigerians... This people majority are your friends*"

"*I was doing business with them*"

"*On a private base or national?*"

"*Both*"

"*If Obasanjo change his mind and decide to expose you and bring you to trial*"

"*Hey...*" his agitation amass

"*Obasanjo can not try that, if he does, he will be lock in a deadly war of attrition with my military-political machine*"

"*Okay you might continue on this after this call*" I press the hold button on the phone

"*Hello*"

"*Halo, una gudivin, una we done o*'" a female voice spoke

"*Good evening madam*"

"*I beg I wan make my own contibute to dis mantar*"

"*Go ahead madam, what is the name*"

"*Eh?*"

"*I dey ass wetin bi yor neme?*"

"*My nem na Groria I dey cal from Ebutu Meta*"

"*I guess Gloria is calling from Lagos, so lets hear her*" I wait

"Okay Gloria tak your side of the tori"

"U si my brodar, Babagida gorment non fevo us a tal a tal, so we non sopoze vote for am again"

"Okay Gloria you don make your point. Thank you for calling. Let hear Mustafa from Paki, Kano. Mustafa hello" silence

"We lost that, hope he calls back" another call is ready

"Hello"

"Hello"

"You are live with give democracy a chance"

"Yes, I will like to make my contribution"

"Go ahead"

"You see I hate when everybody whips Babangida day in day out, I think he is the best man for the 2007 president thank you". I'm happy to receive this call. I would give him the time necessary to convince the viewers. I'm sure Mr Babangida would like to hear him too

"What is the name..." the line clicks into silence. I had asked him his name, where he was calling from and the reason why Babangida is the best man and other things that could had comes up but he is gone. Anyhow, another call is ready

"Hello"

"Hi Felix"

"Hello there, how are you doing tonight?"

"Great, the program is rich keep it up"

"Thanks, any contribution?"

"Yap"

"What's the name?"

"Sorry?"

"Your name please"

"Okus Oromusele from Abuja"

"Here you are Okus"

"Yeah, I had like to say this to Mr Babangida on his comment that if Obasanjo decide to put him to trial, he will be lock in a deadly war of attrition or whatever. I want to tell Mr Babangida that he is not the owner of Nigeria and if Obasanjo or any man could stand to be a man and not a puppet before him, that person will have the incorruptible support of the masses. And your deadly war, I repeat your deadly war will meet the veto power of the nation and your friction will be reduce to frivolous"

"Thank you Okus and it is nice to hear from you on the issue. Give democracy a chance live after the break, don't go away" The commercial break is taking longer than the previous. Many companies and agencies are calling in to air their adverts because about 30 millions people watching the show. The producer hurry me to my sitting position were I'm trying to have an informal chat with Mr Babangida. I had tried to thank me for coming to the program and promised him the show will end as soon as we can make it. It is important he stays to the end of the show. The show's record is unprecedented and the viewing ratio was increasing every quarter of an hour. The light come up and the cameras resume focusing and zooming

"Welcome back, I am Felix and you are watching give democracy a chance. With us is Mr Babagida, retired army General and former military

president and now presidential candidate- election two zero, zero seven".
The camera zoom his face, he is nodding slightly to my introduction.

"You were saying Obasanjo never act to your contrary"

"That is right"

"Does this hold this unpopular move made by your close ally senator
Arthur Nzeribe to investigate and impeach Obasanjo?"

"At a time, I saw Obasanjo going out of line, so I call him...Nzeribe"

"How is my poor Obasanjo now'

"He is good now, watching him closely"

"Hello, you are live with give democracy a chance" I answer a call

"Hello, I am Fatima from Lagos, this is my opinion on the manipulated
Obasanjo"

"Go ahead"

"That freedom is for honest people. No man who is not himself honest can
be free...he is in his own trap, a slave to his own conscience. He is a Yoruba
he will understand my parable. Thank you and God help Nigeria"

"Thank you Fatima"

"Back to Mr Babangida; a source said you warned John Fashenu to
back off from investigating your era if not he is playing a deadly game of
Russian roulette"

"The boy is still deepen his head into the matter despite the warning"

"And the same warning went to England tabloid which covers the
story"

"This people think they are dealing with Blair"

"We will take this call, hello?"

"Hello"

"You are live with give democracy a chance, may I know who is calling and from where please"

"I am Professor Aminu from University of Jos"

"Alright Prof. can we hear your opinion"

"I just want to tell Mr Babangida that his highest mistake is to believe he is untouchable, this his illusional idea has manifested in John Fashenu case which shows we can say no to his autocracy if we are ready not to be fooled again thank you" the line stop and Mr Babangida wipe his nose and dread his face before the camera.

"Aikhomu said as a first speaker in 2002 Jos symposium '...what ever mistake IBB made were unintentional'. Your second and closest in the office then agreed you made a mistake..."

"He was my second but not the closest in office"

"Okay your second man confirmed you made mistakes?"

"Don't mind him, I never make no mistakes"

"An article by Omo Omoruyi said Babangida is a believer in democracy and Buhari a non believer in democracy"

"That is what he said, that is his opinion, so let give him some respect"

"Time ago his comment on you was very negative, regarding June 12 and your restriction on Obasanjo to immortalize the issue and now he is saying something else'

"You know this people, they say the truth just to get attention but when you give them some change, they close their mouth"

"So you gave some change to Omo Omoruyi to say all that?"

"Do you think he said all that in my favor for nothing"

"Omo Omoruyi blamed the recent Itsekiris ethnic cleansing crisis on the Binis and their traditional rulers. He said Oba of Benin and his people rejected the Edowa State in your 1991 proposal. My question is this, is it right to blame the Binis and will the Itsekiris had done better with the Edos than the Deltas. What is the border line in this issue?"

"This issue was raised by Omoruyi, I think he should deal or address the issue himself" at this moment I couldn't find any words to express my mood. Oh this call is a relief

"Hello"

"Hello, hello can you hear me?" the drumming voice ask

"Yes we can hear you loud and clear" I imitate with a drumming tone

"Hello"

"Yes hello"

"Hello, hello" the line click and an engaging tone begin to buzz from the phone's speakers

"Well I am sorry we lost that call, I hope he calls again" I turn to my guest but the phone again...

"Hello"

"Hello, sorry the line went off" the drumming voice apologizes

"No problem, nice to have you back and can you please tell us your name and if possible where you are calling from?"

"Sure! I am Osasogie Edeberi calling from Ekiadolor- Edo State"

"Any contribution?"

"I am disappointed to hear about the article of Omo Omoruyi on Babangida as his candidate. Get this right Felix and the viewers following this program" he coughs and silence follows

"I am not interested in who Mr Omoruyi sides or vote for, that is his constitutional right but check this out, just a while ago in the program, we hear how Mr Omoruyi advised his friend Babangida for the bad government he led, in other words an advice not to run for the presidential post because he is not fit. He ruin our economy, he restrain Obasanjo, bla bla bla" his mockery is like that of basket mouth in nite of a thousand laugh

"See" he laughs again

"Look, it is funny to hear now he is saying Babangida is a believer and another is not. You see, I want to use this opportunity" his agitating voice cracking the phone line

"I want to tell the nation that the chameleon character of Omo Omoruyi is not surprising to anybody from Edo state because he has never contributed anything to this country or his State. Do a public poll on him in this city 99% will tell you they don't know who he is"

"Thank you Osasogie" I cut him off as his slashing on Omo Omoruyi is taking us away from Babangida but another caller is on the line

"Hello"

"Hello, my name is Esosa Omorodio from Benin City" the impatient voice reply

"Please Felix spare me a few seconds for my contribution"

"You are welcome and to hear you, that is why we here"

"Thanks, I want to use this chance to tell Omo Omoruyi and all other self-centered, dishonest friends of Mr Babangida that they protect and promote unfitted man on the expense of our future and the future of our children and their children's children is to condemn him to his own hell and share from that doom. And again Mr Omoruyi can boast he is a friend to Mr Babangida but he cannot boast he has contributed any thing to this nation or his own State. I am ashamed to see Benin, Edo State the way it is when people like Tony Iredia, Mrs. Obasanjo, Tony Anenih, Aighomu, and Ukiwe could claim they are from this State or it's environs. You see Felix, I know this program is not about my State; Edo State..."

"It is about it go ahead"

"This State have all this people in there and all they could do is to stay in their yes sir position and get peanut, the funniest thing is this, they use their peanut from their boss to drive jeep through pot holes and putting on generating plants in darkness around their houses. Everybody with his bad side, this is why I will always stand and raise my cap to greet Mr Osagbovo Ogbemudia. Any thing we look up to in this State today was created by him and the same respect to Chief Igbinedion, I mean the father, not the son, Chief G. Osawaru Igbinedion beside his other side, is a man that knows he is from Benin, Edo State. I will use this chance to tell Ogbemudia and Igbinedion senior to please help people to represent Edo State before they leave the scene. And here is this again please Felix..."

"Take your time I can feel you"

"You see some of this our government people from south-south, they are terrible. Imagine all the influence Maryam Babangida had or and still

has, all she could do with her power was to put Asaba as capital in Delta state. That was all her unchallenging power cold do. Tell me what is the gain now that Asaba is the capital? Does that gives jobs to the youths, does it gives water to the villagers, does Asaba now build the roads and pay teachers and give good health services...please... you all should be ashamed of yourselves. Who cares if Asaba or Asabo is the capital, all I care is good road, education, water, light, hospital, give me this and put capital in grand mother's compound I'm careless. Thank you Felix for the time and God help Nigeria"

"Thank you for your call" I turn to my guest

"More people, groups are coming out for you this day. What is the magic"

"No magic, you see your people like the winning side, they don't care if they are selling their birth right"

"Are they selling their birth rights?"

"Can't you see, oh it is true you don't live in this country"

"So they sell their birth right and you buy"

"I have the money and I pay for their services"

"Who is this Chief George Ezenwa?"

"He is a group leader in Anambra State"

"And?"

"Nothing, he is one of the recent Igbo boys that want some money and I see he want to do anything to get that money, so I recruit him"

"Wonderful"

"That is how it works here"

"Mrs. Bola Doherty from the Marwa fold said you should not usurp the chances of the younger generation and that you should leave the stage for Mohammed"

"Who is this, I don't know her"

"She is..."

"Never hard of her"

"Okay, one Akin Falegan, a prominent Atlanta base Nigerian said in his web site...it is an act of malady for anyone to suggest Babangida to contest an election in Nigeria talk less of presidential..."

"Well..."

"Excuse me, don't you think it will be nice and heroic for you to play a god-father role in Nigeria politics and to be the emperor who watch, gets entertained and give advice rather than a gladiator in Nigerian political arena"

"I will rule"

"With this MUST attitude, don't you think you are insulting the poor masses and provocating them to defend their right maybe by fighting"

"Fighting?"

"A nationalist, one Ogaga Ifowodo wrote on the Internet...'if Babangida become president in 2007, I will exile myself to another country but to return when the cry shall have become 'fatherland or death'. All this predict rash future"

"If it's war, I will war"

"A source said, Gloria Okon was not only alive as discovered by Dele Giwa but she was working for your wife Maryam" he open his mouth and

speaks in silence. He looks around probably wishing this is not on tape. He wait, he had asked who was this source. His face cover with dotting sweats and the issue subdue his patience

"I don't want to comment on this"

"Why?". He wave my insistence away with a head shake

"I don't know how to defend myself on this"

"You made Asaba capital for your wife, why did you create Jigawa State"

"I did that for Hamza Abdullah"

"This Fashenu issue; the 450 billion naira buy-back deal"

"I have warned him..." he stops and changes something he is about to say. He coughs out the fury that burns through his eyes.

"For those who do not know who is John Fashenu..." I face the camera

"...and does not know his connection to this argument and for those who do not know who he is and his involvement in this 450 billion pay back issue, here is a little premise of it" I drag my questioning papers close to my face and I start to read

"John Fashenu is a Nigerian-England base successful sport man. Before the millennium he had a mind to invest in his country Nigeria. He planed to have a shopping mall in Muritala Muhammed International airport. But before he executed his plan, he wanted to know the business and financial situations of the people he was going to partner with. He had wanted to get a real and accurate result. He dreamed he would never have a clean result with the Nigerian investigating agencies he then hired a French intelligence

agent to investigate his future partners. Mr Fashenu through his agent soon discovered that huge sum of money had went back and fort frequently in these to be partners' accounts. When more investigation came up by Mr Fashenu through a high cost foreign investigating agency from Canada, then this famous payback scandal in IBB regime came up but Babangida himself is yet to be touched" I look up from the note.

"At Harvard University Washington DC forums, Mr Robert Milton agreed that if what he did with your government were done in open market, Nigeria would have be richer"

"I don't know all this theories"

"You claim you are a rich man"

"I am very rich"

"Let have this call...hello"

"Hello Felix, I am Turku Musa from Kumo-Gombe"

"Mr Musa, welcome to give democracy a chance"

"Thanks"

"What do you do Musa if I may ask"

"Oh yes. I am a politician, a constituency representative"

Any contribution"

"Yes! That's why I called"

"Right" politician!

"I have this to say to Mr Babangida that he frustrates me when he keeps saying he didn't steal Nigeria money. Who is he fooling? He claims he is very rich, one of the richest in the country for a fact. He was born orphanage and had no economical hereditary, he had a non-money producing career, *no business history. Can he tell the nation where this money's from? He had done what majority of Nigerian will do probably including me but he should accept his wrongs and convinced people he will never go back to it. I will be the first Nigerian to support him but as long as he continues this egotistic dream and 'must' mentality, I would say someone is preparing to stop him. Thank you and God help Nigeria"*

"Mr Babangida... it's not only the civilians that are against you, there are so many retired military officers like in person of retired Col. Abubakar Umar..."

"I don't know him"

"He told New Age News paper that you are unfit to handle the Nigeria first position"

"He can say what ever he like I don't care"

"But we care, the nation that is dying care. The over 100 million Nigerians that lives lower normal poverty rate cares" my voice coming up, I slow to check myself. The producer send me a sign and this calm me. The phone is ringing now

"Hello" I answer

"Hello"

"Hello, you are live with give democracy a chance, your name and where you calling from please"

"I am Rotimi calling from Ijebuode"

"Your contribution please"

"I support Babangida because in his regime he gave money to poor people through the Peoples' bank and he was really a good man. There was

money going round, so I think he is the man to rule Nigeria". Before he hangs up the line, someone is waiting

"Hello there"

"Hello" a tiny female voice echoes from the phone speaker

"Hi there"

"Thank you Felix, I am Nduka, a student- NYSC from Abakiliki, Ebonyi"

"Okay"

"Rather than opinion or criticism, my contribution will be an advice to Mr Babangida but before that I want to make this clear to those who are supporting Mr Babangida that whenever they speak they should try to make a convincible argument. Not just say IBB is the man but you have to say this is the reason why IBB is the man with clear provable, physical evidence. And again Mr Babangida should sit down at home enjoy his loot, his 50 rooms home, his friends and aircrafts. If possible try to use his power to guide incorruptible people to the places they are fits in. I think with that he will be making the greatest success in Nigeria political history. His name will be inscribed in the memories of his fellow countrymen along side with ZIK. Thank you and God help Nigeria". Silence surrounds everywhere in the studio. The silence shades more of Mr Babangida's corner. I'm feeling for him now. I had got up to hug him, to tell him how much I love and respect him and how much I desire his great power for the general will of the nation and not individual will. These are my thoughts but the interview has to continue.

"*This group called the IBB boys, a lot of criticism are coming against them from high place people and they are still canvassing your 2007 return*"

"*I will soon change strategies*"

"*Wole Soyinka asked you to apologize for June 12, I asked this before, I might probably ask again*"

"*Yes*"

"*Why would somebody tell you to apologize?*"

"*He is ashamed to support me publicly as people will feel he is betraying them*"

"*People?*"

"*The Yoruba mostly*"

"*Okay*"

"*Begging me to apologize will place him in a better position to defend himself when he support me publicly afterwards*"

"*You mean Soyinka is supporting you for 2007*"

"*Not yet publicly*"

"*Former Minister, Professor Tam David West said you want to go back to office so that you could subvert the system again*"

"*What is subvert*"

"*In this case... ignore people and the laws*"

"*Well I don't bother myself with people like West*"

"*But I think it's unfair and very, very undemocratic to careless about people who patriotically express their opinions on vital national issues and get ignore just because they have different views*"

"Well..."

"Well you said if Dr. Mbang is God, he could do whatever he likes"

"Yes"

"But..." the ringing phone takes my attention and I decide to pick the call

"Hello"

"Hi, this is Mr Ojukolo, an international business man from Nnewi-Anambra"

"You are welcome to the program"

"Than you, I will like to say few things without delay"

"Go ahead Mr Ojukolo"

"I think it is high time Mr Babangida should stop annoying and insulting people. He has no right to publicly insult people and think he will get away with it. I think Mr Babangida should apologize I know he is allergic to apology but he should and has to apologize to Dr Mbang and lean to respect people who are more fitted to the presidency position than he"

"The maritime operators recently blamed you and your then vice Augustus Aikhomu saying, because of your corrupt government, foreigners continues to dominate the nation's oil lifting"

"I make more money with foreigners"

"You were the special guest of honor in Sunmi Smart Cole's Photo News Magazine launched in September 2004"

"I have being wanting him to work for me since I meet him in 1989 in Europe"

"Work for you, how? he is a Photographer"

"I know his job, I need a good photo image in the public and more now that he have a photo news magazine"

"In 2001, many Nigerians abroad especially those in the USA were annoyed with the office of Colin Powell and the American government in general for issuing you and Buhari Visas through its' representative in Lagos" He is listening with calm interest as if he is hearing the story for the first time.

"...the visas were protested with an open letter to the office of the secretary of States through series of human rights and democratic groups" he wait to hear the question

"Well, don't you think these are signs you are not accepted to be president again or at least not at this time?"

"A lot of people don't like my good work but I will be there"

"There is this book you wrote...'For Their Tomorrow We Gave Our Today'"

"Yes it is my selected speeches"

"It cost about 40 US dollar"

"About that. I could check it up with my publisher"

"That is more than 5 thousand naira"

"I don't change money"

"The public can't afford that"

"It is for those who can read it"

"The people's rejection about the idea of your coming back to power is even display in the home videos. Gbenga Adewusi's 1993 work 'Maradona', also know as Babangida must go is a full picture"

"Home videos are for the Onitsha boys, that's not politics"

"Mr Kanayo Esinulo, a public commentator said '...anyone who wishes Nigeria IBB at this stage deserves a psychiatric attention. That is quiet a message?"

"Let them wait in fear"

"This reminds me, the Okigbo panel..."

"Don't let us go there again"

"Why?"

"He was a NADECO agent"

"Who?"

"Okibo was collaborating with NADECO"

"In the eve of August 27 1993, you had many State files, tapes and many secret filming moved from Aso Rock"

"Yes"

"Where are those files, they belong to the State"

"I know but they are in my custody"

"Alex Ekwueme is now your errand boy in Igbo land"

"I need someone there and he doing a pretty job"

"No matter how the pressure will come from the public, Obasanjo will not probe you"

"He can't, I gave him 1.4 billion naira to campaign and other things I did for him"

"In October 2004, a British rapist out of prison won 7million pounds in lotto extra draw and you commented that it will be the same luck you will have to win the 2007 election"

"Yes"

"Is so weird for a presidential aspirant to inspire his dream from that of a rapist image"

"That is what God can do"

"The June 12 is not a personal thing"

"A lot of people take it personal"

"They don't. They only express their rights...We have to take this call from Biu, hello?"

"Hello"

"Hello there you are welcome to give democracy a chance. Do you mind telling us your name and where you calling from exactly?"

"I am Alhaji Danguoma from Biu- Borno"

"Okay"

"I will like to express my feelings to Mr Babangida that I am sensitive to this his moments. I will express my respect for his courage to stand all the moments but I will admire him more if he accept he made mistakes and realize being a president is not a do or die affair, thank you and Allah help Nigeria"

"Thank you Alhaji I hope Mr Babangida listen" I turn to face Mr Babangida

"You said June 12 shouldn't be an issue"

"It shouldn't"

"You..." oh the phone

"Hello" I answer

"Hi Felix, I am Olu Jide, national news paper editor Victoria Island Lagos"

"Right Olu go ahead"

"I have few words for Mr Babangida. He is paranoid when people talk about June 12, but I wonder why people cannot talk about it. It was a day the whole nation went to the 110 polling booths to say yes and you single handedly and said no and you made that your no to stand above the nation's yes. Not only the insult you gave to the whole nation, more than that, the country suffered terribly...United States our biggest oil customer suspended most aids and sharply cut military training programs with us and stopped other assistance. So I think there is a need for Mr Babangida to sit down and think of the general will and not his personal will that continue to be his priority. Thank you and God help Nigeria"

"Thank you Olu for your wonderful contribution and I hope Mr Babangida takes a little rather more time to reflect on all this because it is better to be thought as a person and not as a personality". His face looks tire, many things probably going through his mind at this moment. He wants to say something, maybe leave the studio though his two hours agreed time has not expired. One thing that has not betrayed him since the program started, is his calm mood except the occasional agitation from irritating questions and viewers' comments

"A lot of foreign annalists who studied your performance concluded that you are better qualify as a coup maker rather than a president" he laugh

"I want to be a president"

"That is fine by me but a president has to qualify for it"

"I am qualified. I made myself qualify"

"When Abacha died, the whole nation celebrated instead of mourning"

"That was their feelings"

"Now that a lot of people publicly show they are against you...against you not as a human being, not as a Nigerian, not as a Muslim but as you being the president. Don't this gives you a kind of concern especially when you saw the way Abacha was and is still remembered"

"Of course it worries me but I think I can work my way to their hearts and they will sing my name"

"How do you want to be remember after death... celebrated or mourn"

"The end will tell... Let me tell you once more, the only people I pity in all is the Nigerian public"

"Why?"

"Because anything that happened politically in this country only the public suffers. People keep talking about June 12, June 12, June 12. Look at the people that were at the front role in the 1993 democracy fame... starting from Abiola himself when Abacha seized power what did he do, he openly expressed his support to him. What about Baba Gana Kingigbe, Iyorcha Ayu, Lateef Jakande, Adamu Ciroma, Tom Ikimi, Bamanga Tukur they all ran from democracy rally to serve in Abacha's cabinet". He looks at me like what is your next question

"Wow" I manage to say

"For us, when I say us I mean we up there. We know how the game is played, that is why I don't listen to these mouth makers. Once you give them what they want, they change mouth. This is Nigeria"

"Oh this reminds me of one of you up there. I can remember exactly who. He said every body up there including himself should be taking out of Nigeria polities and government offices"

"Yes, yes Idiagbon"

"Oh he said that"

"Yes"

"How did you see that as a solution"

"No comments"

"They can even stay and make it work they just need to change their minds to truly serve their nation and that will make the great difference. Change our mentality and be patriotic"

"I know what you mean"

"How was Idiagbon?"

"A great, fearless soldier with good vision"

"You agreed with him only the incorruptible youth will bring up Nigeria"

"Sad to say but it is more of true than lie"

"Why can you stand to be the role model, the hero by bringing these fitted youth in and take out the 'you' up there"

"I don't know". Phone ringing

"Hello?"

"Hello"

"Give democracy a chance, hello"

"Mrs. Obademi from Akure- Ondo"

"Let's hear your view Mrs Obademi"

"I think Mr Babangida can really transform this country, He can let fitted people go in there. I know you can do it Mr Babangida if you choose to. Base on your childhood, I think you should stand for the poor, the homeless, the orphanage, the oppressed, stand for that humanity your childhood had robbed you off. That is the best thing you will do for your country and the most valuable thing you will do for yourself thank you and God help Nigeria"

"Thank you Mrs. Obademi That was very touching I am really moved by your motherly words I hope Mr Babangida feel the same emotions I am feeling right now, thanks I really appreciate that contribution"

"Abacha wrote a script for an indefinite extension of his personal rule"

"From there I started suspecting him he didn't want to leave the office again. Then in 1995 Obasanjo-Yar'Adua coup came up, later in August 1998 the then five registered parties choose Abacha as their candidate. From there I was convinced this man meant business

"So what happened?"

"I waited, followed him closely then Diya was gone with alleged coup"

"A lot of people worries, the majority of Nigerians says if you can not do anything positive in 8years as one man power leader, what can you do in 4 years as a many man power leader?"

"I will and must continue to do what I do best"

"Abiola said he came to you more than five times and you promised him you will leave office and that was why he ran for the presidency"

"Truly he came to me"

"Why did you then threat him like that"

"But I didn't really want to leave the office"

"You were playing, fooling every one in the nation"

"I wasn't fooling anybody"

"You claimed the reason for the annulment was for irregularities"

"I needed to say something to justify my action"

"Majority of big people didn't believe you, even Obasanjo then called your excuse...let me use his words...'spurious'...he said your excuse was spurious"

"Obasanjo has no fitting to say anything"

"The Encyclopedia Britannica article said the hope raised by your political-economic reform was not realized. It went on more directly... 'The regime leader (IBB) clung to personal power and frustrated expectations of political evolution, self-seeking and a loss of political direction'... That is really a huge failure levy on you"

"I don't listen to all that"

"People says Abacha was a leader of circumstance"

"He was, I trained him to be one of Nigerian most feared soldier"

"Sorry to answer this again. In the VOA Hausa Service interview was this famous 'only God can stop you from being the president in 2007 what do you mean by that"

"That is not the words I used"

"Fine but that was the message?"

"Yes, let say yes"

"Let take this call from Jebba-Kwara, hello?"

"Hello good evening to you all in the studio. I'm Ibrahim Manta, formal lawmaker in the second republic. I will like to remind Mr Babangida a few things in a democratic State. It is a pity he lacks knowledge of the constitution, he won't have said only God can stop him. The constitution can stop him as well. Let me give a simple example, he is been accused of human rights violations during his regime, let say Obasanjo is pressurized to probe him and at last he is found guilty of the account. Definitely he is going to serve the punishment...prison, death or as the law may decide. If this happens, which is possible, then how will your only God can stop you promise be fulfilled" Mr Babangida is not responding to this, I can tell from his straight gaze.

"Your political bureau in 1987 attested to the high level of corruption in your regime. This was their words '...corruption pervades all strata of the Nigeria society from the highest levels of the political and business elite to the ordinary person in the village'"

"I know why I setup that corruption Committee"

"Why?"

"Just to mollify the public"

"You are really working on Obasanjo"

"That is our deal"

"Reliable source said Obasanjo administration refused offers by experts to trace money loathed from Nigeria to overseas during your regime?"

"He has no choice, he is in the game"

"But he supported Abacha's investigation"

"Yes that is because Abacha is dead, he won't try it if Abacha was alive"

"According to a renown economist, Professor Anya O. Anya fears Nigeria economy is showing critical sign of distress. Inflation in September 2002 was 14.8 percent, industrial utilization was 41% in October the same year"

"I was not there in 2002"

"Foreign reserve declined from ten billion in December to seven billion naira today. These decline are all linked to your regime"

"I am not an economist"

"The UNDP said in 2002 over 70 million Nigerians has lives below the poverty level"

"Nigeria is a rich country"

"There is an increase of over 30 million since 1998, rising the people living below poverty level to over 100 million"

"I don't know this..."

"Just a second, we take this call and then your time to continue...hello there"

"Hello"

"Hi there you are wel..."

"I am calling from Lagos, I am a medical practitioner- LUTH"

"Right"

"I always dream to serve my country and live here in Nigeria but the situation in Babangida regime forced me out of this beloved country. I

was away though God saw me through to become a successful doctor in the United States. I am happy for Nigeria democracy, I am happy to be back in the country to use all I suffered in foreign land to help my nation. But it is not okay with me to allow Mr Babangida again to come with his strategies to take away the little we have built in this fragile democracy. If he happens to come back in 2007, my friends and I and our family will return back to the country that had given us so much respect and values. Thank you and God help Nigeria"

"Better life Nigeria association"

"Yes that was the group I organized to disturb the 1993 election"

"Chairman of the national Economic Intelligence Committee professor Ibrahim Ayaji said you ruined the Nigeria economy"

"I have sent another professor, professor Abdulahi Michael to reply him"

"When you took over in 1985, Nigeria owned creditors 27.5 billion dollar and when you left office in 1993 the amount increased

"Yes"

"Now you claim you repaired Nigeria economy?"

"What did you expect me to say"

"Say the truth"

"The truth indeed"

"Abiola was your friend so also his 1993 opponent, the millionaire banker Bashir Othman Tofa"

"They were both my friends, we all play gladiatorially in the same arena"

"You confirmed Abiola came to you to ask if it was okay for him to run for the presidency?"

"Yes he came"

"Then you betrayed him at last"

"I told him if he runs, there will be a problem but he didn't listen to me"

"Abiola repeatedly say you encouraged him and promised him you will leave"

"I told him there was going to be trouble"

"So you knew there would be a problem even before the election was held "

"Yes"

"Why did you lie to the public and fooled every one in the nation, you were spending billions on election you knew was not going to be held while your fellow citizens were without food and shelter" I breath sorrowfully

"I was doing my best...even when he was there as a president he wouldn't had lasted for six months"

"Why?"

"Because he wouldn't have made a good government"

"There is a call, let quickly take it and come back to this issue... Malam Adamu from Ibi- Taraba hello?"

"Hi Felix, compliment for the program"

"Thank you"

"I just want to make Mr Babangida see how he keeps contradicting himself and making a huge fool of the nation. He admitted Abiola came

to him, he was there during the formation of parties, He formed them, the money spent, the election stress, now he said Abiola wouldn't had make a good government. You knew it all, you knew he was not going to be a good leader and you were luring Nigeria to it. And to my surprise you claim a defender of human rights. You knew trouble would come, you knew Abiola wouldn't had lasted for six months, you knew all that and you carried Nigeria to it and we still suffer the effects, nationally and internationally. I think Mr Babangida has a better work to do at the moment than to fight for president. He needs moral rehabilitation till he is ripe from his inner heart to truly serve his nation. And lastly, I want to tell Mr Babangida that to truly serve your country you don't need to be a president before making history in your country. You will be my hero if you realize, it's best to be thought as a person and not as a personality. Thank you Felix and God help Nigeria"

"Thank you for your contribution but before we give words to Mr Babangida, we will quickly take the waiting call...hello"

"Hello" the waiting voice replies impatiently

"Yes welcome to the program. Your name please and where you calling from"

"Mohammed Turku Alfa from Kumo- Gombe"

"Go ahead"

"Thanks Felix, I just want to add to what the last caller contributed..." the line cease.

"Hello? Hello, well we lost that. I hope he calls back" I look at my questionnaire

"Gani Fawehinmi said you use your security chiefs Haliru Akilu and Col. Tunde Togun to blast journalist, editor of NewsWatch magazine, late journalist Dele Giwa?"

"Look when the blast happened, I told my boys to arrest Dele Giwa's wife but the media noise was too much that no one saw what I planed after the bomb explosion"

"Recently, you influence the sacking of Chief Don Etiebet, head of national working committee through the Sokoto State governor Attahiru Bafarawa's friction"

"I don't waste time with people who are not serious"

"And you supported and guard other ANPP governors headed by Ahmed Sani Yerima to remove Etiebet"

"I do anything to remove an idiot..."

"It seems Aikhomu has lost confidence in you"

"Really?"

"He did not come when you invited him on Etiebet- Bafarawa plot"

"That is his issue, what I wanted was done without him anyway"

"Why did you remove Etiebet?"

"You see, Obasanjo's a player, I found out that the only way to secure Northern president is to use the ANPP but Etiebet was there"

"He needed to be removed"

"At all cost"

"This reminds me, you said Idiagbon was a man of vision"

"He was"

"Why did you obstructed him from realizing his dream?". His answer is not coming instantly, he is thinking, looking a little above the height of an athletic

"Idiagbon was having his goals and I was having mines"

"What happened to him?"

"In or out of office, we are inside the arena for always"

"And..."

"And no player takes eyes away from you till you are gone"

"So Idiagbon was..."

"I don't know" he cut me off. The producer signals me for time off. I glance through my wristwatch... about forty minutes left for the two-hour time show.

"People call you Maradona and Abacha a bully. How was he able to maneuver you and took his name from the list of the officers you retired before you left office"

"He didn't. I personally allowed him to stay as I have said earlier" I'm not getting the answer. I have to move to the next question

"In 2005 Democracy Day celebration, Obasanjo in his speech outlined most things he can't stand, among many is intimidation. In his words" I turn to my questionnaire

" '...in my age, I will rather die; all dis bad belle people'... who was he referring to?"

"When death comes, we all will die, each at his own turn"

"When Chinua Achebe did not honor his award, that was a big blow to the government?"

"Ask who is ruling. In my time, I won't worry myself about that"

"Buhari is still having his election issue in court?" he shrugs to say, that is history already. There is nothing one can do about it. A call

"Hello"

"Hi there"

"Compliment Felix. Wonderful program"

"Thanks, please can you tell us your name and where you calling from?"

"Sure, I'm Iyabo Adetusa, a final year student in international relations -EDSU"

"Would that mean Edoversity - Ekpoma?"

"Yes, yes"

"You from Edo State?"

"No. I'm schooling there but I am from Ikire - Osun State"

"Right. Any contribution?"

"Yeah, as a Yoruba, I want to say we should look for another person to represent us. President Obasanjo failed us. We are all, I mean majority of us are disappointed. In his six, seven years, no one can stand up and say this is what Obasanjo has done for Nigeria. Let be real, he may have set up commissions and committees like the NDDC; development project in Delta region but nothing works with them, nothing at all. Obasanjo biggest effort in the last six, seven years is on corruption but the irony is, corruption have grown with shocking percentage in these period. A sensible person will conclude thus, if corruption has been fought these years and the result is increase and not decrease then one thing is clear that, the government has

encouraged corruption and never fought it. You hear people been arrested for crime but after bribing, off they go. If a house of REP member the house speaker for that matter: Salisu Buhari can forge a graduate certificate and became a ghost graduate from Toronto. Or the obscure investigation of Senate president E. Enwerem, tell me what we expect from the government such individuals represent? E don tay wey dem dey chit we poor citizens. 'We don't want a soldier' the people cried, 'ok' the man said. He pulled his green uniform and puts on a brocade kaftan. He is the same thing he only changed his shirt. The people want the man to go not his dress. I read in a paper yesterday, a millionaire and a Nigerian diplomat's son jailed in UK for robbery. My course mate said to me, '…what a life do I live as a millionaire and a diplomat having a son jailed for robbery', 'that's why we shouldn't dream to be like them' I replied. It is obvious that nothing will improve with these same names. The fallibility of Nigerian government is perpetuated by the silence, the refusal of the commoners to act. We should have a new start with new, young people. There are many out there only that these old names will never allow them. Thank you". She drop her phone and before I turn to my guest, another caller is ready

"Nashiru from Lagos hello"

"Hi Felix. I call to comment on the issue the last caller raised"

"Which is?"

"The disappointment of the Yorubas in President Obasanjo"

"Oh yes please"

"First, it is not only the Yorubas that are disappointed. It's the whole nation. In fact majority of the Yorubas are not disappointed because we

didn't support him in the first place. I would personally say that President Obasanjo tried, he has done good, only that good is not good when better is expected and best is possible. For me it has nothing to do with Yoruba, Igbo or Hausa, it is our leaders from day one in 1960 to this day. Nobody ever represented the Yorubas. Our value has been exchanged for greediness right from the time of Cocoa farm to Ota farm. Historically, our leaders prefer to fight themselves rather than uniting. From the time of Kankanfo Afoja-Alafin of old Oyo to Awolowo-Akintola in 'Action Group', a melee that led to the 1966 military coup. See Abiola-Awolowo in 1979 election or Obasanjo-Falae 1999 duello or Adams- Fasehun on super voodoo OPC leadership. When Obasanjo came in, in 1999, he did the traditional first day at work enthusiastic employee, convincing himself to work 24/7. In a Jack of all trade mood, he called Chukwudifu Oputa and Mathew Kukah to heal Nigeria's ail; starting from 1966 coup through Abacha's massacre to Abubakar's last contract awards. After seven years, all is still smoke with no fire. He ended making a deal with Abacha's family instead of rigorous check and retrieve he promised"

"Hello" another call

"Hi Felix, how're you doing?"

"Could be better. You?"

"Great"

"Name please"

"I am Lizzy Nduka Ogunkoya"

"Nduka Ogunkoya..."

"Yeah. I am Ibo married to a Yoruba"

"Profession?"

"A broadcaster and TV presenter with NTA Kaduna"

"Wazobia colored to the full". She chuckle

"So lets hear the breaking news Lizzy"

"Uh…" still struggling with her chuckling

"As Nashiru said, if you look at our politics, it is obvious that the problem is our leaders. Once they are there in the office, they force all systems to operate their way. They will transport their families and acquaintance to the 'moon' and make them sleep in palaces and ride in flying horses. Common men they will send with guns to kill their political opponents or those that don't share their ideology. They sit down and think of themselves, invent anything to loot and loot. I dazed when I read lawyer Mike Ozekhome's declaration that Obasanjo spends over a billion naira on tea and coffee in every two months. That is inanely fatuous. Our politicians now try invents a matrimonial-hood amongst themselves, a conscious attempt to legitimize feudal nobility. This is an effort I foresee to have a horrifying genealogical complexity…"

"Lizzy…"

"One more thing Felix"

"Yes?"

"Ask me why Maryam changed the Nigerian police uniform…"

"She did? Anyway this is opinionated and …"

"Felix, they spend millions on millions to sew this black and black calico that only the sight of a police in the uniform is a night mare. I would love if the government can answer these simple questions, this Police

uniform, what change has it brought to Nigeria? What was the necessity? Was the Police uniform that needed a change or the Police mentality? God help Nigeria"

"Woo"

"One thing justifies our leaders' constant hoarding of money in foreign banks. It shows the symptomatic of their endemic insecurity in a country they call their own, thank you" the phone stops. I can't waste time. I've to ask my own question before another call

"So this presidential third term constitution rumor is real?" I ask the guest

"I don't believe it. Who ever makes that move will be putting his feet on a war zone"

"Obasanjo said people keep calling him for third term"

"Nobody calls, he is calling himself"

"The Okibo report was finally published at last sometime in 2005"

"I think I read that too in the papers"

"There was nothing in it but long passages of confusing English, so verbiage"

"People let you know what they want you to know"

"Nigeria is one of the World most corrupt countries, how do you think you are going to deal with this?"

"I will do it"

"Obasanjo in his eight years..." phone interrupt

"Hello"

"Hel…lo" the voice rock faintishly and after several beeps, the manly voice steady with static clarity

"Hi"

"I am Garba from Gboko- Benue"

"Garba is working right?"

"No! Not yet, just finished a degree course"

"Oh congratulation, degree in what?"

"Medicine"

"Hey doc.". He laughs

"Go ahead"

"Mr Babangida is saying he is going to do this and that. I feel these are all only words. We the suffering citizens need facts, Obasanjo wasted eight years fighting corruption and now it is even worse than when he began. His governors and ministers are being arrested overseas like some street burglars. You want us to live on your name for another eight years or more. What are we expecting this time? You need to tell us, show us, and convince us. What we need now is different from what we have always got. We need an idealist not a consumer. We have laws to guides us, so that we won't be under anarchy but no one obeys laws in this country. So why spending millions in making laws if no one follows them. It's fine the top people handle the money. That's why they are there anyway but the money has to work down to the bottom level: the Reagonomics and Thatcherism in the 70s are good examples. The youth is ready to fight, not a physical fight but a mental one. Running to abroad we thought was an answer to our plight has now turned to be our nightmare. Thank you"

"Thank you Garba" I turn to Mr Babangida

"The Nigeria green passport is so uncared for that Britain and many other European countries are putting on ban on Nigerians visa applications. That is so humiliating, isn't it?"

"For me, I will go to anywhere I want"

"We have Chioma Oche on the line. Chioma hello?"

"Hello Felix"

"Hi there"

"Thanks for taking my call"

"Thank you for calling. Sorry Chioma can I ask where you calling from?"

"I am calling from Otukpa- Enugu. I think it's time we the poor citizens start telling the leaders of their errors. Look at the America medical team that came in voluntarily to help our country. With no payment, they carried out major surgical operations with cost the patients' relatives never had afforded. What happened? Because of our greed we spoilt this christianed hearts term-work and made their efforts worthless with fake drugs and killed- murdered patients that may have survived the operations. And the head of the hospital, though with a cultured-humble dignity, recognized he had no reason why he shouldn't know what was going on in a department he heads. But the fact that he didn't know what was going on in his hospital is a fatal, unacceptable working attitude that deserves sack or prosecution. What country are we if a teaching hospital head don't read national newspapers. Surprisingly, Minister Ola Lambo? was so insensitive to great lost as the one in Enugu teaching hospital that he put up an arrogant defense to cover up

his negligence. As embarrassing as this issue stands, Obasanjo's government refused to call the people involved to account. Professor Lambo told the BBC....'well, let them present the matter to me again with a formal letter before...'. Before what? Gosh! Innocent people died in the hospital on the ground that involves hospital negligence, all a minister of health could say is, let them write me again before I do something about it. In this fatal, negligence of the government and devastating pain caused to the families of the victims, the health minister's resignation is the least the public should be asking for and indeed the ministry as a whole should be charge for murder or at least for manslaughter. Obasanjo's government needs to do something about this faux pass before it leaves office. God really help Nigeria" the line end abruptly and a momental whirr turn into diminishing beeps

"Hello" another call

"Hellooo, this is give democracy a chance and how are you doing?"

"I'm okay Felix, thanks for taking my call"

"It's our pleasure"

"Emm...". Babangida looks away to catch one of his old speeches from uniform now playing on the studio-television. He will pay as high as 100 thousand to the TV if they will agree to stop showing this footage... at least for this moment. He watches in his usual melancholia: a spirit of intellectual exultation and maneuver rather than a paralysis of regressive depression.

"Would you like to tell us where you are calling from and your name please"

"I am Ete Ekpan from Yenagoa- Bayelsa"

"Right, let me ask you this. Do you agree with the argument that youth involvement in the government will improve Nigerian politics?"

"There is no doubt about that Felix. I'm convinced that any good, purposeful politician will agree with me that youth is the wheel in which a nation's progress rotates and I'm sure Mr, rather General Babangida will agree to that too..." the camera show Mr Babangida, he is following with relax attention

"...I feel that youth has been abandoned by the government for so long and there should be a new start with the youth as a center of attention. Old name in whatever form - civilian or military is old wine..."

"Mr Ekpan..." I interrupt

"Just a moment Felix if you could..."

"Go ahead"

"Thank you. Our problem is, we don't have leaders to look up to, no heroic leaders except Zik that comes to my mind at the moment. We cannot have a good government if our cabinet members are fraudsters and our governors are prisoners. They all caries doctor or professor before their names, it arching and frustrating to see non of them could prove they deserve these titles. It's very hard to choose from any household names in Nigeria. The so-called icons have all worked for the forces that later became their doom. Look at Abiola, we cry of his June 12 denial but he was the one who sponsored Babangida against Buhari. At last, it was the same Babangida who showed him 'pepper'. See Ken Saro-Wiwa, during the civil war, he escaped from Biafra side to joined the Federal and was appointed civilian administrator of oil port in Bonny till or even after General Ojukwu

fled to Ivory Coast in January 1970. In 1987, he directed MAMSER for Babangida and supported Abacha discarding Shonekan in 1993. What happened at last, the same Wiwa became the Federal government's enemy, the enemy he fought till his November 95 execution. Abi na Awo - Awo who was rumored to had poisoned himself or by someone after his boy Jakunde set him up to the military that he was conceiving a coup"

"How do you think the youth can take a central role in already established power of these ex military who are not ready in any way to give up the power?"

"Historically, there is no place people have given up power just like that. Youths should start letting their voices heard in a peaceful but determined way"

"Who, how will this start?"

"Individuals, groups teaching self awareness, citizens' responsibilities, we must not forget that, all the changes that have taken place in human history always start from the minorities - from the bottom. A break in an established order is never by chance but opposing force calling the established to account. You know, a change needs sacrifice and we Nigerians quest pleasure with no sacrifice. We youth will take the step to stand and face these old names. I think lots of women are ready to help in the change"

"Before you go, any word for Mr Babangida"

"I feel I have made clear my position. To tell the public you can rule them, you have to present your conviction from a podium of objective pyramid of truth and facts. Thanks and God help Nigeria"

"Thank you. Before the next call, let me ask Mr Babangida this" I flip over a page in my questionnaire

"You claim you donated more money into MKO Abiola's presidential campaign than any of his friends"

"That's correct"

"Why at the end you cancelled what you supported and financed"

"People would have criticized me if I had handover to him"

"This didn't occur to you when you were putting money into the campaign". A vivid irritation wrinkles his forehead.

"You live with give democracy a chance. Fumilayo Omotola from Lagos hi"

"Hello"

"A student?"

"No, I am an international business woman with a small business in England"

"Okay, what is your view on today's topic?"

"My view on Nigeria situation in general is very negative. Nigerian government is not doing anything. The politicians are blinded with selfish gains that they just simply destroy the nation. For instance, see the national identity card the government has being working on for decades, right from the time of minister Shagaya to the present day minister, ask them where is the money meant for this ID card thing? It is not only Babangida or Obasanjo, all of them. I do not think I'm far wrong, if I'm wrong at all to say, I support the 30-70 years political age and I support all the ex-military and politicians dreaming public offices MUST be cleared through

incorruptible commission before taking part in any government election. First, we must change the way we practices our politics or else anything, any plan, any project, any committee form will never work. We the youth need to take rebuilding the nation as our pride. To govern is to serve. This is my advice to all our politicians from the post of the president to the post of ward councilor to go and find out the meaning of the word SERVE. Thank you"

"Thank you for your contribution. The number to call eight eight one six four four three seven two, the charge is ten naira and keep the calls coming. Stay with us, we will be right back after the break. IBB live in give democracy a chance" the commercial comes on. A mobile phone company exaggerates their new pay as you go service and a Dutch-beer convince workers how nice it is to chill out with their product after a hard day.

"Welcome back and now on the line, is Mamud Abdulahi. Mamud hello"

"Hello Felix"

"Hi there where are you calling from?"

"I am calling from Bantaji- Taraba, I lives in Japan though"

"Oh long way from home uh?"

"Yeah,"

"So how are you seeing the Nigeria situation?"

"Sad, really sad Felix. I am convinced if nothing is done about our present situation, Nigeria will be one of the poorest nations in Africa in near future. Because our leaders are only consuming, taking the public offices as their personal investments, this is our problem. Nigeria has what it takes to

be in one of the World richest and developed but we need planning. Imagine Ghana now see by Western World as the road map to West Africa. Watch this out, Ghana and Malaysia got their independence from Britain in the same year with the same economical background but when the BBC made a comparison of the two countries in June 2005, the Ghana president; J Kufor himself confirmed the incredible gap Malaysia have left for Ghana to cover. Malaysia now competes in global marketing while Ghana is still praying for investors to come to boom its economy and IMF to cancel its debts. You can imagine Nigeria's fate if at the moment, Ghana developing standard is 14% greater than that of Nigeria. Look at Nigeria itself, Nigeria – Indonesia; tell a similar story – oil, military rule, population, ethnically diverse but Indonesia average income has moved from $200 in 1974 to $680 in 2001 but in Nigeria, opposite is the case. Thank you" the line clicks and I turn quickly to my guest before the phone ring

"Let say the worst scenario of this uncertainty, say you eventually bluff the opposition of overwhelming majority of Nigerians and move ahead to become the president, how do you plan to revive the decaying economy?"

"First, I will agree with you that the economy is really in a horrible state. My plan will be to create room for foreign investors" I look into my note for a question but the phone is ringing

"Hello?"

"Hello"

"I'm Justin Chukuma. It is aching, very sober to hear our leaders thinking foreign investors will be the 'Christ' to take away Nigeria's sins. It is an idea, a good one indeed for investors to come into a country for *economical boom. Do you think investors are blind? They are not. Nobody sow in infertile ground. If investors come in, we have more money right? Is it money we lack in Nigeria or the knowledge to manage it? I think the latter. These skiving politicians..."*

"Skiving?"

"I have worse Felix, yes skiving, mitching, foraging, butting, gulling..."

"Whoop, whoop, whoop, okay! We heard you..."

"Except a country have..." he continue

"... a spirit of prosperity, no investors pays interest. If otherwise, Obasanjo six-seven years' dream for foreign investments would have been a come-true thing by now. Came 2003 election, all we got was three military candidates: puppet Obasanjo, Buhari and secessionist Ojukwu and the race, biasedly refereed by the almighty Babangida. The best thing General Babangida should do for his country at the moment is not being a president but guidance to the young selfless minds to truly serve this country with absolute freedom. Thank you"

"Thank you Justin and a caller from Edo State are you there?"

"Yes"

"Hello"

"I am Dave Okuromi from Ishan speaking tribe of Edo State"

"Ishan..." trying to remember Ishan on the map

"Where Tom Ikimi and the rest are from" he helps

"Oh yes"

"They are from there but nothing to show for it"

"Profession?" I jump the instant polemic

"I am a writer and a publisher"

"Go ahead with your contribution Dave"

"In my opinion, the failure of Obasanjo is unprecedented. I know he has or he's trying in his own way to improve Nigeria, no doubt about that but the results proves that he has no political capacity to govern. In fact, he confessed at the beginning… the CNN live broadcast of his 1999 inauguration. President Obasanjo said he is not Jesus Christ and miracles shouldn't be expected from him. Yes, I quite agree with the argument that one man cannot solve Nigeria's problem in a week, fine! I'm convinced that the president in a good faith to his office and to the nation has done what he considered best in all State matters. My argument is evidently; nothing plausible had been done in his six, seven years in government. I had expected at least, a sign of where the country is going. Even the president cannot tell us at the moment where the country is going. If the corruption rate was 70% when he came and now corruption rate is about 96%. Some people would say this government don't know what it's doing, they pretty know what they are doing. They pay heavily to build and secure their safety, mould walls and razor-wire gate around their family. But our roads, streets are plague with darkness, potholes, open sewers and some tiny, tiny OC-Police people with disheveled uniforms and repair am make i work guns in the darkness leaning against battered black pick-up van only to harass and kill vulnerable citizens they are meant to protect"

"Thank you Dave for your contribution"

"One last thing I would like to leave with the youth"

"Sure"

"Weep not youth, weep not my fellow youths. The conquest of our identity will remove our pain. The ravening clouds shall not be long victorious, they shall not long possess the sky..."

"Woo, that was Walt Whitman"

"Yes, resurfaced in the opening of Ngugi Wa Thiongo's weep not child"

"Dave playing in his terrain"

"I will take that as a compliment" he laughs

"Of course, it was. Thanks again for joining us"

"Thank you for having me"

"Give democracy a chance in a moment, right after the break, stay with us" the commercials come and go

"Welcome back..."

"Hello" another call

"Hi"

"I'm calling from Lagos"

"Name?"

"I'm Nancy Thomson, actress and producer in the Nollywood industry"

"Right"

"On the Police issue in this country, it's a double tragedy. Police is like half cast; it's not white, not black. It receives whip from the government who employ it and betray the public it's employed to protect. Police in this country strip innocent citizens and turn to guard the thieves to their razor-wire villas. In return it receives miserable salary- peanuts"

"It looks like, police is a victim of both side"

"Yes, yes it is…not friend to the public and gains nothing from the government"

"It can join the poor citizens to put the government right"

"Ahaaa! Now you talking, but police don't have that sense"

"They don't know they can arrest anybody irrespective of his or her official position"

"Police arrest politicians in this country? Oh you think you are in America where a police Sergeant could pull over a State governor or President to be for over speed and give him a ticket. This is Nigeria, where politicians are gods. Police arrest bus drivers who don't have money to bribe because their vans lack one headlight. Police arrest young school leavers because they walk in the streets with no jobs. Go to our prisons, you see fifty to sixty people cram into 10x10ft room for months, years. Who are these prisoners? There are hungry men who stole chicken and bus drivers who carried ten passengers instead of eight. Woe to these police men and women; not really the police on the road blocks, I mean the Oga them who abuse their power and wreck the lives of the needy they are meant to protect and abet the evils they are to fight"

"It is a shame"

"It is indeed. At times, I stay and ask myself, who are we really to look up to? If Wole Soyinka can be stopped and refused entry to a country *like South Africa for immigration irregularity, then our struggles have no hope"*

"But it's almost normal these days. We hear our governors and ministers been arrested, banned from countries"

"Yes, our governors and ministers can be arrested or banned, I can expect that, it won't surprise me at all because of what they are but not Soyinka, no! Not what he represent us to the outside world"

"You sound depress about this"

"As a matter of fact Felix, it was a personal defeat for me"

"Oh poor you"

"I know"

"Thanks anyway for calling and good luck for your best actress nomination for this year"

"Thank you". The line cease and I turn to the guest

"Nigeria is the most religious country on earth. Things ought to be different with our faith. For instance, you see a Church in every third house in a street"

"The religion aspect of the country…" the phone again

"Hello" I answer

"Hello"

"Welcome to give democracy a chance. How are you joining us"

"I am ok Felix and you?"

"I am doing good. Thanks for asking"

"I'm Temitope Ogunmola, a professor in theology- IWO School of Christian Doctrinaire"

"Right professor"

"I was hoping you touch this aspect in such a profitable program. I am glad you did because this aspect is foremost, barely after corruption in today's Nigeria strife"

"Are you saying religion is the cause of our problem?"

"Not religion per se. But the way people are putting definition to it. Church in Nigeria has become nothing but a proliferating selfish business, new denominations springing up in every six hours. Now Nigeria has the highest Christian denominations worldwide. A` la moda now in churches is Marriage committee"

"What is that in the Bible prof.?"

"They arrange husbands for the desperate aging wives to-be and pimps, sorry for the term, for that is what it is, the pastor pimp wives for made-it men..." I start to laugh with Mr Babangida

"Hold on to the drama. Before you sign the marriage contract, the committee will visit your house, inspect where you live, if you have cable TV with AIT, silverbird, channel and if you can watch the American Jerry Springer show or listen to CNN news"

"All these to pass marriage exam?"

"If you are to make money in business Felix, you have to sell quality products"

"Unbelievable"

"Unbelievable but real. Then your car... and you have to submit you bank account to the committee for balancing"

"Here you go, that is the main thing. Bank account is what is all about"

"Hang on a second. After four to six months, the divorcing couple starts dragging the pastor for claims, why? The prepackage he sold is fraud…You see, I cry for what awaits us when the Lord comes. Not all churches…but overwhelming majority, I say 99.9%. Thank you and God help Nigeria"

"Thank you professor, I hope we all reflects on this". As he hangs up, his shrewdness sends a shivering emotion inside me. I turn to my guest looking through my questionnaire

"Abacha placed you under surveillance and in 1998 he is alleged to had tried to assassinate you"

"But today who is dead?" his reply shows a buried victory of a suffered battle. He reflects for a moment and sink into a surly shush

"You said you will never return to politics" I galvanize

"Yes that was then but I never ruled out politics completely"

"Now we have Martins Okoje on the line. Martins can you hear me?"

"Hello Felix"

"You are live with give democracy a chance. May I ask where you calling from"

"From Sapale- Delta State but I live in Canada"

"Right, any contribution?"

"Yah, I would like to conclude what my fellow citizen Dave Okuromi was saying"

"Dave?"

"Yes, the publisher from Edo State..."

"Yes, yes please"

"I am saying thank Goodness, Obasanjo's time is coming to an end. I wouldn't stick myself on the failure issue because it is too late to cry..."

"When the head is off" I help

"I should be more concerned about the future, that incompetent leaders should not handle positions that determines the welfare of over one hundred and fifty million people. I am afraid this is the same reason I am not in favor of Mr Babangida to rule Nigeria... We need to have proofs and be guaranteed the country's fate will be in the hands of person or persons who knows what the citizens want and he or she is ready to do it for them without compromising. And women should be given more chance in the government. The little chances they got over the years have been a great success. The NAFDAC's Dora Akunyili war against fake drug is an outstanding example. Titi Abubarka and Eki Igbinedion's struggle to restore womanhood, though with no historical result, but it is worth emulating and lot of other wonderful women out there in the public offices. Thank you".
The line cease and I look into the camera

"Give democracy a chance right after the break, don't go away". The commercial comes on and I have chance to have a word or two with Mr Babangida before the producer do the count down himself.

"Welcome back" I flip my questionnaire but the phone...

"Hello?"

"Hi"

"Compliment Felix for the program"

"Thank you"

"Please do this often, it is very interesting"

"I will deliver your request to the production unit"

"Thank you and I want to say this, that Mr Babangida should be a belonger of this country and not a owner of it. He single handedly decided Abiola should not rule when the country's majority said yes. He single handedly placed his brother there afterwards, he single handedly dusted Obasanjo there. Interestingly, he wants to single handedly put himself in now and again. Mr Babangida is my idol and more if he takes a wiser decision Thank you". I turn to my guest to ask him a question from my head but the ringing phone is insistent

"Hello"

"Hello"

"Welcome to give democracy a chance, name please"

"Tude, Tude Olumide calling from Shagamu but I reside in Scotland"

"Very well"

"I want to say it's time for the youths to stand up and speak for themselves if they want to have a future. I think we have realized that running abroad or joining cults in schools are no longer a means of escape from the decaying situation but a means of condemning our future. Imagine Africans in British prisons, 37 percent are Nigerians. Statistics shown by an independent European organization says 40% West Africans prisoners in Europe are Nigerians…"

"Uh?"

"It is unbelievable Felix and it is the useful age of 15-45. So it is high time, a constitutionalised political age should be 30 - 70 years. Except the youth come to our rescue..."

"What do you mean by youth coming to our rescue?" I intercept

"The youth age of 15-45 years, are shipping themselves abroad and these sadly, are the ones that have been through some sort of education. Now they leave the country for the junks and the cult people to rule. What do we expect at the end?" the question sound rhetorical, yes it is

"... intellectuals don't govern with cultism and godfatherism" he add

"I agree with you"

"Thank you, so unless the schooled youth stop moving abroad and face a tough battle to rebuild this nation, things will hardly change. Now you hear new terminology from the politicians... geo-political zones! Especially the South-South politicians, they use this to fight for more money so they can have much to mould themselves into gods"

"So what do you think about IBB 2007"

"What do you think I think?" we both laugh

"I don't know, you tell me"

"I admire Mr Babangida but I don't have any convincible reason or reasons to support him at the moment.

"Hello" another call

"Hello, you are live with give democracy a chance, how are you doing?"

"I am doing great and you?"

"So well thank you for caring, name?"

"Madelyn Uche calling from Aba- Abia State"

"Let us hear your view Madelyn"

"I would say we are living in a new era, we need new ideas, new minds, not necessarily new people which I recommend anyway. For a change, the old names shall pass away. 'You can not put new wine into old bottle' said the grand master otherwise the bottle brakes and the wine waste. Babangida should stand as a mentor in Nigeria democracy. A lizard prepares its second journey to the treetop, if the lizard thinks very well it will be obvious that if there is a treasure on the tree, it had found it the first time. Mr Babangida should see this reality from President Obasanjo's failure. The answer should be, before Obasanjo leave, he should make this political age and embezzlement-free certificate for the 'ex' into a constitutional act:

"Hello" I answer another call

"Hello" the caller replies with an in-born Mancunian accent and a formal silent follow

"Your name please?"

"Edward Adebosun" his words sharp from a nasal intrusion

"Mr Adebosun is not living in the county right?"

"Not really, I'm British of a Nigerian origin, in fact from Ekiti"

"It's clear, your contribution please"

"Thanks Felix. First, I would like to say hello to General Babangida..."
Mr Babangida nod lamely as the camera zoom out his face

"...I am a professor in political science, University of Manchester. I would say from my personal view that all Nigerians living abroad would like to come back home but you can't blame them if at last they don't. It

is abhorrent that African leaders, especially Nigerians still hold this selfish tradition that government positions are roles you fight for and get by all means for personal usage. Tony Blair sometimes ago was to buy a house, his second or so, it was a national debate for months whether, why, how, when he is to buy the house. At last he bought this self contain home he will pay in a period of time. A prime Minister of one of the richest countries on earth..." the telephone crack and I pray inside me not to loose this line. After several cracking hellos, the voice steady again from the phone speaker

"Yes professor, sorry about that"

"That is alright..."

"Continue prof"

"As I was saying, a Nigerian president, minister, governor or local government chairman not to mention the least, only a year in office, he will buy ten houses in France, eight in England, six in America, five in South Africa...you can go on with the rest" laughing from the crew and the audience but Mr Babangida is not amuse.

"...at the end, they are all incarcerated in the prison of their ignorance and stupidity" silence return

"I have seen that..." the professor continues

"...it is the youth of this nation that will make Nigeria's dream come true and I support the move that the constitution should be amended... forbidding the ex, ex people both military and civilians with former public office record till they pass through incorruptible screening committee before standing for any government office. And for Mr Babangida, I assume he has majority of opposition, he will be having more forces to deal with when *in power than anything to contribute to the nation. I wonder what he has to gain to risk himself into tribulations again instead of being a moderate mentor that carry Nigeria democracy into the hands of true servants. Thank you and God help Nigeria"*

"Hello" another call

"Hi, give democracy a chance, how are you doing?"

"I am doing well Felix and you?"

"Fantastic and thanks for asking"

"First, I would like to say compliment for the program"

"Well the compliment should go to the producer, thanks anyway I appreciate"

"It's brilliant"

"Thanks, name?"

"Kunle, Kunle Ogundipe, from Lagos but I resides in South Africa" his words lace with a cadence of an eccentric Lagosian knight

"Lovely place uh?"

"Yeah"

"What is Kunle doing in Mandela's country?"

"I am working and at the moment concluding paper works for my neutralization"

"Becoming a South African?"

"Yes"

"Why?"

"You know why Felix. I had no hope at home and I moved. You see, unless there is a change and new young incorrupt minds leads with general

will spirit. Imagine governor Tinubu will now start contesting for president when he has done nothing as a governor. I mean, he said the other time '…use seat belt when driving or you get ticket.' Seat belt in ten kilometers per hour? Is it seat belt that causes our road incidents or potholes" he waits, maybe for an answer. None is coming

"Is it flood or gutters, open sewage across the roads?" he pause

"When they come up with new ideas to siphon money, it's like fire in the mountain. Seat belt o! run, run, run. After two or three months, the idea dies because the money has been shared. Who talks about seat belt today in Lagos? None! The roads colonial masters left, are still the main roads we use today. The governor addressed seat belt, don't he know how many hours it takes to cross 3rd Mainland bridge? He cannot address that, can he? It's so ridiculous when you see names sitting at the back of these V boot Benz or so often now, you see them inside these latest air-conditioned SUV, 4x4 - Off Roaders with vanity plate numbers like… Oba this of that, Obi of that, USA 1, Daddy, FCT, bla, bla" he laughs in a piteous tone

"Nigerians with bogus names. That's my people for you. At times, I pity myself and the other youths looking ahead the distance we need to walk. But I'm not scared, the journey has started and up we will match, we…" the line crack and the voice stop

"Oh we lost that. Okay lets take the next call from Owerri, hello?

"Hello"

"Your name please"

"Obina"

"Right. Your contribution?"

"*Yes, on Nigeria corruption, I feel the problem is the illusional glamour we hold, that Nigeria is the giant of Africa, the 'this' oil producing country in the world, the this, the that. Nigerians have high taste; they want to live like the Americans. The truth is, the Americans suffer a long term, take one step at a time to be where they are now. But the average Nigerians would love to jump from one to ten. It is only a corrupt, unintelligent mind that would want to acquire the moon without scratching a finger. Blaming everything on the government is ill judgment, what about the citizens, are we playing our roles? We want good government, are we ready to take the right path for the good government? Before Columbus first stepped into the Americas, see the sea he needed to cross. Before the whites came to steal our fathers and our gold, see the voyage they fought through. Before the black Negroes became liberal Africans/Americans in the USA, look at what Luther King Jr. Malcolm X and others like Rosa Parks went through: Rosa Parks- the Alabama black lady who refused to stand up for a white passenger in a city bus. She was charged and fined $14 but her bravery changed America racial history. Before South Africa became apartheid free, ask Mandela what happened. If we Nigerians want a good government, we must first be good citizens and fight to change our ill ways, thank you*" surprisingly, Babangida applause.

"*Koka from Ibadan on the line. Mr Koka hello*"

"*Hi Felix, how are you doing?*"

"*I'm fine thank you. Tell us more about yourself*"

"*I'm Bidemi Koka and I am back home now, I lived in the USA for sixteen years with my family*"

"You are back with your family?"

"Yes, we arrived two years ago and my youngest son will join us at the end of this year after his graduation"

"So how is life back home?"

"Not like in America I must confess but here is my country and I need to stay and contribute in my little way to build it"

"Your profession Mr Koka?"

"I am a surgeon and my wife is a business product from Harvard"

"Woo"

"We are here with our two lawyer daughters"

"What is your opinion on Nigeria situation?"

"Well, it is like every other developing country. Obviously lots of things are not in place. We all have to make the change. This task falls on everybody, especially on the youth but at the moment, all fingers need to be pointing at our leaders who are doing too little or nothing of what they ought to be doing. It is unintelligent that our leaders are waiting for G8 world to cancel their debts and build Africa economy. This is an illusion that will never come through. It's like a thirsty trotter pursuing a mirage in the Sahara desert. Often we will have some non-governmental minds that will make noise about Africa debts or poverty or AIDS with good intension though but at last, it's investment for them. Look at the 2005 live 8 concert in G8 nations; the highest ever put on stage for Africa aid, till this moment, no African street citizens knows such thing ever happened. But many European web site companies made millions from Internet ticket sales and journalists made careers and the media made headlines and singers promoted their

albums. Westerners will never make our economy level theirs. Why would they do that anyway? If they do, how would they control our oil and gold and diamonds? How can they tell us the quantities to produce and how much to sell them? It is possible the world levels economically, after all, World population is less than seven billion but Bill Gates personal assets worth over $40 billions. Well, he supports humanitarian projects, ok! The Wal-Mart family worth $100 billion... My cynicism on western efforts to Africa development is aflame by the implausibility of its mega bureaucracy to the effort itself. In medical advancement, over 1,500 drugs have been introduced in the past 25 years, not more than 20 out of these 1,500 drugs can treat tropical diseases. In the last decade of the 20th century, over 70 billion dollars went into medical research, guess what happened? Less than 400 million of the 70 billion was directed to diseases of the poor as the western calls them...aids, malaria etc. Western World (America to mention a name) can give billions of dollars to NASA to photograph some stones in the Mars or in the Jupiter, but when there is tsunami in Sri-Lanka or houses quakened in Pakistan or famine in Sudan, they can not send more than some cartons of milk and some blankets"

"Western World agenda is to see Africa grow and you are saying..."

"Sorry to interrupt. I am not saying anything contrary rather... if we can not develop ourselves, the West is very, very I repeat very, very reluctant to help us"

"I know what you mean"

"The Americans or the British don't dump into solving your problem if there is nothing to maneuver. The British argued that the American Puppet;

Augusto Pinochet is too old to stand trial for his crime against his citizens in Chile. Den dey old pass retribution? Washington can send Madam Albright or Colin Powel to draw the road map that will stop the reprisal of Sharon against the Intifada in West bank. But they insist doing nothing but the OAU leaders should convince Mugabe not to destroy his people's home"

"It is very easy for us Africans to blame our problems on the West as you are insinuating and..."

"No, no, no, no, far from it. I'm saying we should take our responsibilities and work with sacrifice for the kind of life we want rather than sitting and looking for scapegoat. Nobody is going to give anything for free not even your freedom. The European slave trade abolitionists preached for more than 70 years but not until Samuel Sharp revolted against his master in 1831 inside the Caribbean sugar cane plantation that the circa 300 years' man inhumanity to man began to head towards a collapse. We can build this country (this continent) without waiting for the Western. We have the resources to do it. Nigeria don't need aids, it needs law, positive opposition parties, decent civil service and the know-how to run its own businesses"

"This's Nigeria version of the South African Moeletsi Mbeki on Africa... init?"

"I'm a fan of the Mbekis" the camera zoom Mr Babangida's face

"See this Felix, between the oil boom in the 70s through the Abacha's cardiac infarction to date, the nation have received more than $650 billion, I won't mention the IMF loans or other foreign aids ... with all this, Nigerians are three times poorer now compare to the 70s when the oil doom began. Our debt now is about $40 billion. Nigeria at today stands

one of the world-lowest per capital incomes. Banned goods still come into the country with the same quantity before they were ban. Now 87% school examination malpractices compare to 30% in early 70s. Corruption increased to 96%. In 1999, World Bank rated Nigeria 13th poorest country in the world. Sadly, today we are among the ten world's poorest. 65% of Nigeria youth is scattered over the globe. In fact, nearly all countries in the world have a Nigerian community" The line crack

"Hello?"

"Hello, yes we can hear you Mr Koka"

"Okay, I conclude with this, I mean it's we Nigerians, who will make this country the way we want it. The recent 50 billion US dollars debt relief that favored Nigeria, apart from in the news, what other signs has the government show to the citizens that such thing ever happened. In Nigeria, we think we know what we know but we know we don't know what we know that we should know"

"Don Rumsfeld?" I ask and he starts to laugh

"You are really from America" his laughter makes everyone laugh

"Thank you for your contribution"

Thanks for allowing me to share my view" the line end

"Before the next call, let me ask Mr Babangida this question" he raises his head toward me for attention

"You said in a paper recently..." I look at my questionnaire

"...something like... who said thunder can not strike twice?"

"Who can be sure?" he shrug and rearrange his hands on the table

"You said Margaret Thatcher and Abiola advised you to run as civilian president when you were in power but you said no because you will be operating in a different environment. 'I am used to given orders' you said and ' can't go begging or lobbying for people to listen" he listen in a catatonic gaze

"How would you rephrase that now?"

"Well…" he gaze to the ceiling in an obscure emotion as if he is going to free himself from the words that will descend

"Our next call is from the East, hello"

"Hello"

"Hi, name please"

"Helen Ogukwanu, I'm Idoma. I work for the Ministry of External Affairs"

"Any contribution Helen?"

"Yeah! I called to add this on the last caller's western attitude towards developing nations. See, I was talking with a colleague yesterday in the office, she said in the middle of the conversation…'can you believe the British government refused to have Nelson Mandela's statue in a London square. I am not surprised I told her. If you follow history, this refusal will prove yet again British government's hypocritical sympathy to developing nations' heroes. When Nelson Mandela's birthday celebration came up in the mid 80s, Margaret Thatcher' government said Mandela was a terrorist and to celebrate his birthday is glorifying terrorism. Not long before the partition of India and Pakistan, Wilson Churchill described pacifist Mohandas K. Gandhi as a skinny, half naked troublemaker. To me, the whole Mandela

statue issue in London is redundant, uncalled for. He is not British, never fought for Britain, why is his statue being politicalise in Britain? Mandela fought for Africa. His statue should be in Nigeria, Togo, Kenya... All 54 countries in Africa. Thank you"

"Thanks Helen. Now lets take the next call from another professional. He is a retired army officer- 4 mechanized brigades Abuja. He is retired brigadier Ike Nwanfor"

"Hi Felix"

"Thank you Mr Nwanfor for taking time to call"

"It's my pleasure"

"You are retired, when are we expecting you in politics". Laughter from the other end

"No Felix. Politics is not made for everyone"

"But you are a retired army"

"I know that. Army is not a transitional profession to politics"

"Oh I thought it was in this country". Silence, he felt the bite

"I mean..." trying to repair if I damage anything

"I don't support ex soldiers dominating this country's politics. I tell you what- that Nigeria politics is rigid by the overwhelming presence of the ex military. We even have more army Generals and Admirals and Commodores than police cars and Obasanjo's six P's are our holy grail"

"And you think we can overcome this"

"Yes, yes. There is no way a soldier can nurture the perfume of democracy, it will conflict his professional beliefs. To eliminate this army structure

from our politics will be a perpetual and more rigorous objection from the bottom- the commoners"

"The fact is commoners needs people like you to speak out more often"

"I agree with you"

"Mr Nwanfor I'm afraid we have to leave you here and thank you for your time"

"Thank you for having me"

"Hello" another call

"Hello, welcome to give democracy a chance"

"Thanks for taking my call. I called to add a quick word or two to this wonderful, thoughtful program"

"Thank you. Name?"

"Bello Elkanami. I'm a farmer from Zango, Katsina"

"Good"

"You know, people use this mentality of kill and divide Nigeria. When they can't have enough or more than what they hope for, if they can't get that god position, you see them becomes paranoiac, See Alhaji Dokubou who worked so hard in Obasanjo's campaign for an agreed reward. When he couldn't get what he hoped for, he selfishly declared his own country. You see..."

"Alhaji Dokubou should have asked Ogukwu for advice before embarking on owning a country"

"He didn't get anywhere. I mentioned this just to point out one of many examples.

"Your view on IBB 07?"

"If you ask people, say who do you side in the presidential race? You will hear many saying Babangida"

"Why?"

"They will argue that during his regime, he ate and let others eat. Kill and divide, you know"

"Is this positive for the nation? We are still suffering from his last kill and divide, you know"

"I know. I didn't say me. I said people. You see, now that election is coming people have started flocking slavishly into Babangidaism without an iota of his ideas or his policies. They don't care but only for the kill and divide dream"

"We appreciate your view and thanks for calling" I face the camera

"We will hear Babangida's respond to this in a moment after the break. Stay tune"

"Hello" another call after the break

"Hi"

"Compliment Felix"

"Thanks"

"My name is Opara Chukwu from Igbo-Uzo but I am on vacation from America planning to move home finally anytime next year.

"Mr Chukwu let me ask you this, how hard it is to leave a place like America to come back to Nigeria where...I mean things look a bit tough"

"That's a good question. Well, it all depends on individuals. It is really challenging"

"What are you going to do when you come?"

"In my life, I've always taken one thing at a time. I'm to move in here then what I will do will come to me with good devotion to general will. I wouldn't mind starting with a community service when I come"

"Your view on the nation's progress?"

"It's moving though the result is too low to see a visible progress. I think the youth will be a source of revival if they take part in their government"

"Why is every Nigerians living abroad feels the youth is the best alternatives for Nigeria leadership?"

"First I don't believe is every Nigerian living abroad hold this opinion and to answer your question, It's very simple, our older leaders have corruption as custom and tradition and they are not flexible to changes. But youth though corrupt are flexible to changes and they are growing to match the computer/information age"

"But there are lots of youth who goes into politics and becomes more corrupt than the older politicians"

"I would use the word contaminated. A youth will go into politics with good intention but he or she has to pass through party obligations and cult rituals and pay allegiance to superior politicians. So when he's there, he is force to forget his mind and follow obligations that only match his sponsorer's needs. Look at the Anambra State Ngige-Uba tussle for example, a bully art that produced and directed the dilemma of Okija shrine. I have couples of friends who moved back home from The States and Europe to join politics with good intension but after a year or two, all I hear from them is how to transfer money to foreign banks"

"So you support this 30-70years political age?"

155

"Absolutely, I will really recommend it. Again, let me clear this. The role of youth we are talking about is not that all ministers and governors will be twenty years old...no, not that at all. Let see America and Europe for example, public opinions counts a lot. Public opinions affect government policies, this make them rule themselves, it makes them part of the government but in Nigeria, nobody knows what is public opinion or it affecting the government's policies"

"Thank you so much Mr Chukwu for your contribution and looking forward to seeing you back home"

"Thank you. I would like to use this chance as an honor to say hello to General Babangida" the camera zoom Mr Babangida's face while he acknowledge the greeting.

"Let me take this chance to ask this" he smiles

"You said the 15th January 1966 failed coup that killed PM Tafawa Balewa, Ahmadu Bello, his wife and many northern officers changed the nation till today"

"Yes! It made the Northern officers felt insecure. With the Ibo and Yoruba education, we knew the only way to have say in Nigeria as North was to go the hard way"

"Hassan Katsina, then commanding officer in your squadron preached this 'hard way' to you and the rest junior officers like Abubarka and Abacha"

"Yes, I remember him saying 'coups succeed coups' that was how it all started"

"For you it became clear that the 66 coup was Ibo against Hausa"

"Sort of"

"Was that why Operation Araba coup organized?"

"For two things I believe; one for revenge and the other Northern control"

"So…" the phone…

"Hello"

"Hello"

"Hi Felix"

"Hi there. You are live with give democracy a chance. First, let me ask you this, do you really believe, youth abroad will play a good role in the government due to their exposure to good political society?"

"Yes, I strongly believe that we the youth abroad will play a good role in educating others from the grass root but this is more of individual than abroad thing. Youth at home are invaluable as those abroad. I think, in my opinion that it depends on what individual wants to do for his or her country irrespective of their residential status. Over the years, especially in this present republic, many Nigerians came back from America and Europe to join politics here at home but at the end they are more corrupt and have more foreign bank accounts than the old politicians. We want the youth to start speaking out, hear words of this author: Chika Onyeani in his book Capitalist Nigger - 'the road to success'. I recommend it to the youth" he pause.

"Thank you"

"Thank you for your contribution. We will take the waiting call and come back to Mr Babangida" I look up to him before I pick the waiting call.

Oh I forgot to ask the name of the last caller… anyhow lets hear Amina Shehu from Kebbi. Amina hello?"

"Hello"

"Yes, you are live with give democracy a chance"

"Thank you for picking my call, I will like to give my opinion on how possessive our leaders are. They are convinced that holding a political or governmental post makes you the owner of that post, example of Minister Rufai giving Federal capital's lands to Enyimba football club players for winning some Africa club cup. Don't get me wrong, I'm a good fan of Enyimba and rewards for players are good and encouraging but, but" he cough

"… Enyimba is a private entity. If it were the Eagles fine! …because these are for the country and the land idea must be debated and voted for by the houses. Can you imagine Gordon Brown, the British Chancellor giving London Hyde Park or Trafalgar Square to Liverpool or Manchester United just because they won the UEFA Cup or Condoleezza Rice of USA. Can you imagine Con-Dolce Rice giving the Los Angeles Lakers the Pentagon Airfield in Washington for winning the American basketball championship. Or say Silvio Berlusconi given the lands around the Coliseum in Rome to AC Milan for leading Serie A or playing the Europe Champions league. I am happy anyway that Minister El-Rufai gave these lands to at least Nigerians who own their land. If na only dat wan dem fit get from their government, it's not bad. If NFA and all other national sport management bodies owning athletes air tickets refund, this will tell you how pathetic our authorities are. It's horrible even more if our leaders believe debt relief

is the miracle. President Bush during the 2005 G8 summit in Gleneagles -Scotland said, 'Why would I take tax payers' money and give it to the countries whose governments are corrupt?' The war president is damn right I said to myself. See one of our female Ministers…umm, oh I can't remember her name now"

"Me either" I look at Mr Babangida. He returns my look with even if I knew, I will never tell you

"Anyway…" Amina continue

"… she is there giving contracts to her relatives?. And she still had the guts to say she wants to sue the news paper that investigated and brought the happening to the public" he stop

"We need to restructure our priority through real education. Thank you and God help Nigeria"

"Thank you" I turn to Babangida

"Now, Mr Babangida, America closed its embassy in Lagos recently because of terrorist threat. Where is this leading us to…I mean, our relationship with the outside world?"

"Sincerely, I don't know. Obviously Nigeria needs renovation from A -Z" his mild tone concealing the physicality of callers' irritations

"Hello" another call

"Hi"

"I'm Alhaji Bello Tafa"

"Alhaji's profession?"

"I'm a religious leader"

"May I ask where Alhaji is calling from?"

"From Gusau- Zamfara"

"Okay Alhaji, thanks for calling, any contribution?"

"Yes, I would like to comment on the free trade we believe is our savior"

"Right"

"First, I am glad Mr Babangida agrees Nigeria needs renovation from A-Z. They tell us only free trade with the Western will rescue us. West on its own is no fool, free trade would mean loosing its economical power to Africa. With Africa's raw materials, good weather, abundance cheap labor, Africa world market domination will come in a speed of light; Africa's cheap, better product will leave no room for Western manufacturers - the 2005 China-EU textile quotas duel is an example. And again, free trade might not change anything because what we have for the world market are mostly raw materials and raw materials have under-value till they are processed. We don't have the technology that will transform these materials into more value products. In free trade, we are going to sell under-value product, my point here is free trade can't do much if we are not developing ourselves, thank you"

"Thank you Alhaji" the line ceases

"The next call is from Solomon. Solomon?"

"Hi Felix"

"Hi there. Solomon right?"

"Yes. Solomon Ruaa from Jos"

"Any contribution?"

"Yes Please"

"Go ahead"

"On the corruption issue and what Obasanjo government called anti-corruption commission- the EFCC. The head of this commission Mr Nuhu Ribadu bragged on a BBC interview sometime in 2005. These were his words '...if you think you can steal Nigeria money and enjoy it in London or else where, you are lying...' some crap like that. I want Mr Ribadu to come out in a public media to defend his words when public figures in person like my State governor Mr Joshua Dariye could steal our money and buy home in rich London street worth 300, 000 British pounds and have over eight separate bank accounts. He was arrested in UK, breached bail but Obasanjo anti corrupt commission is asleep as the governor continues his usual in Plateau State. Let Mr Ribadu defend how he dealt with Kema Chikwe; OBJ's bitch that ruined the Nigeria aviation to desolation or Lady Anajemba Euro's check or the Bayelsa's state governor, Mr Diepreye Alamieyeseigha UK authority bust. We hear in the papers, so and so is arrested for fraud or embezzlement but after a day or two, stori end. The offender have paid...paid, you know what I mean, don't you? In the papers, you will read...sentenced to two years. Trust me, she will not spend two months. They will say... the government have confiscate, seized their properties... seize wetin? I beg e! The government banned textile goods but the so-called government people, their wives, girlfriends, children wears designers from 'Italy'. The banned tomato paste in their kitchen's locker will show you the 'exceptionalism' that malfunction Nigerian laws. The Nigerian government is so good mastering its capo lavoro: corruption. Anytime one of its members revolts- always for selfish reasons, the government twist the rebel into a

scandalous setup to bring back normality. It is treacherous of the government rather hypocritical of the ruling party to sack IG Balogun, set up governor Alamieyeseigha or investigates Uzur Kalu out of personal aggro putting on the pretence mask of fighting corruption. What about Ibori or Attah? The most bizarre of all these set-ups and scandalous international arrests is that things never change. After two weeks, arrested governor returns to office and continues his 'usuals'. Let just pray for God's intervention, thank you and God help Nigeria"

"Hello" I answer another call

"Hello"

"Hi there, how are you joining the issue?"

"Just addition to that of my fellow citizen who said our hope is within us and not on western"

"Yes"

"Look at the national derivation fund. It works the other way round. We shouldn't believe in Obasanjo who is lured in a matter of convenience, into dreaming that western hypocritical paperwork will help Africa or Nigeria let say the least. The thieving Nigerian nationals are alleged to have above 50 billion dollars in banks outside the country, mainly in Europe and America. If we own 'you' 40 billion and at the same time keep 50 billion with you, Felix you make an argument out of this..."

"Not me". We all laugh out

"The IMF..."

"Right but..." I interrupt

"Excuse me Felix..."

"Go ahead"

"You know, you don't need a Cambridge degree to understand why Bill Clinton withdrew his troop from Africa after not more than sixteen soldiers were killed in their peace mission and Bush refused to withdraw his troop from Iraq after loosing thousands of soldiers and still losing in their led invasion. Britain and Germany are aware of the ruination of the Royal Dutch and Shell in Nigeria. Nothing has been done about it and trust me, they will never as far as the oil keeps flowing. Who to blame? I am less concerned about the western consumeristic quest. I am more dreary or lugubrious on the corrupt African (Nigerian) leaders who I side the western to call Homo-africanus"

"Right"

"Thanks Felix"

"Your name please?"

"Saliu Abusalah from Nguru- Yobe"

"Thank you Mr Abusalah"

"Give democracy a chance in a moment, after the break, stay with us" the commercial break is short

"Welcome back"

"Dele Giwa, before opening an envelop marked 'from the office of C in C'; a parcel that would kill him, he said 'this MUST be from the president- you" another silence but soon realize it won't work. An answer is better no matter how blurry it comes.

"He could have mentioned anybody's name"

"Maybe Halilu Akilu. His last caller who asked for directions to his house less than 24 hours to his death" he gazes at me in a noisy silence

"We will be right back, give democracy a chance". We comes back from the break with a waiting call

"Isoken Cole from Edo Sate, hello"

"Hi Felix"

"Hi there. Edo Sate right?"

"Yeah, Benin City but I live in Milan - Italy"

"Italiana, ciao"

"Salve"

"So?"

"First, I would like to comment on the last caller's argument especially the one on America. I know this program is not about America but I find it sad seeing, hearing people beating over and over again this America who do everything to better humanity more than any country in history. America fights for their interests just as all other nations… see that America donates aids more than any nation in history. It sends its soldiers and humanitarians to wars that are not theirs. They fight for other countries freedom and democracy. America invests in projects that benefit the whole world. America is a country where freedom is at its highest and other cultures and beliefs are accommodated. I feel that most modern anti America feelings are nothing but jealousy, fear, intimidation of a prosperous, welcoming, freedom preacher country. Despite our feeling, we are all obsessed with this God's own country. Not to loose the track Felix, allow me to come back on the issue of our leaders taking office as their inheritance"

"Good"

"You know, this is due to the nature of our politics in this country. You see, politicians fight their way to positions in a do or die battle. Whenever they win, the victory is taken as a personal effort and he or she as the case may be is indebted to himself or herself and only those who contributed to the victory. In the office, they don't have any sense of been chosen by the people, in fact they are not. So you don't expect me to explain my traveling to you when you didn't send me any message. This reminds me of the caller that talked about our leaders obeying party's obligations and allegiance to godfathers. This is Mr Lucky Imasuen in my State...this man came from America with the motto of 'change' and serving the masses. In his campaign, he boasted and promised to pull down the corrupt gate of the government. The Edo State masses followed him and when he saw no instant gain, he abandoned the masses at the middle of the road and sojourn in the house of those he earlier condemn. Today, Mr Imasuen guards the government's gate he promised to pull down" she stop

"It is very atypical of democracy" I reply

"I know, that is why, not until we citizens start to elect our leaders, they will never represent us, thank you"

"Thank you for your contribution my young lady" I want to ask her what she is doing in Italy but I let her go. She might know what she's doing there, judging the way she spoke

"Give democracy a chance, right after the break don't go away" the commercial is taking longer and we pass glasses of water round

"Welcome back. Now lets take our next call" I press a hold button on the phone beside me

"Hello"

"Hello"

"Who is with us?"

"I'm Nosa Edokpolor"

"Where is Nosa calling from?"

"From Okada- Edo State"

"Wonderland!"

"I'm calling to have this said that President Obasanjo should be given some credits. This is a civil war veteran who recuperated and managed a government distorted by counter-coup, jailed by his junior officer and now trying as a civilian president to revive the nation. I mean some praise"

"The President should have some praise. I personally agree with you. Thanks for your call and lets go with the next call" the hold button again

"Hellooo! George Menuagbe, George can you hear me?"

"Yes, yes I'm here. Thanks for taking my call"

"It's a pleasure"

"The program's wonderful"

"Thank you, profession?"

"I'm a journalist, political editor- THE NATIONALE

"Right, what is your headline George?"

"Rather a message to my co journalists and the journalism in this country. The fear or the convenience not to point fingers to the worms that eat this nation sore my beliefs in this profession. Because Abacha is dead and

everybody picks up pen and writes his atrocities. Who said all this when he was alive? This Abacha man ruled for five years and what about Babangida who ruled for eight years and indebted Nigeria. I have not seen any military regime worse than that of Babangida's. Abacha intimidated people, killed people. He inflated physical pains you can leave behind and move on as a nation. Babangida inflated all of Abacha's and more economical wound that the nation can't leave behind to move forward. What about Obasanjo's eight years maladaptive policies, let leave his infamous 70s military rule aside. In his book: This Animal called Man, an ironical title full of religious hoax comforting itself in the gullibility of the helpless citizens whose hope on the 'oil' is like a moon fading into a far horizon. At some point in the book, one feels he is reading a synagogue work of T.B. Joshua or that of the Canaan land Oyedipo. What are we saying about this people now? Abacha followed the footsteps of his predecessors. Our journalistic cowardice is waiting. You know when to talk, when the accused cannot reply, that time, what good are your accusations to the nation? We write mountain of stories against Abacha now, of what use? Slovo said…'The world (I mean Nigeria), would be a poorer place if it continues to be peopled by children whose parents risk nothing in the cause of social justice for fear of personal loss'. At the moment, we write and report incommensurably on state matters, a journalism that continues to leave our audience with satirical dissatisfaction. Babangida is the last person to come up for presidency at this moment. As this Canadian writer: Marq de Villiers depict the 07 dreamer in one of his books 'Into Africa' '…the military took over again under General Ibrahim Babangida, who started building dozens of grandiose projects- the World's largest this, the World's best that and within a few years, the country was bankrupt, with an annual deficit exceeding $4 billion…"

"Just a moment" I intercept snappishly

"Someone could say, yeah, you made your point against Babangida fine! But hang on a minute, I'm a citizen too and I want Babangida to rule"

"I will respect his or her view but he or she needs to back up the argument with reasons. Is like you say to me, I need this dog. Fine! Why do you need the dog? Is it because you will use the dog to scare the farmer from his farm and take all his yams or because the dog is your pet and it will protect your house from intruders. Which one?"

"I'm speechless George"

"So would anyone who will have such baseless argument. Thank you"

"Thank you George"

"Hello?" another call

"Hello"

"Yes, give democracy a chance"

"I am Mary Ediren" a young female announce sonorously

"And where is Miss Ediren calling from?"

"Mrs.… I'm a Belgian resident but a Kokori speaking tribe from Delta State"

"Sorry about the incorrect title"

"Don't worry, it's not getting you in trouble"

"I am relieved" I say jokingly and she reply with amazing laughter

"You live in Belgium?"

"Yes, I work with a Belgian NGO in Brussels"

"Can you, would you like to tell us more on your work with this association?"

"Yeah sure. The association is back by the European Union Commission for African human trafficking and human right abuse"

"Yeah"

"I called to have this said on this important topic"

"Oh yes go ahead please"

"According to statistics in Brussels, Nigeria is the highest country with its citizens scattered around world prisons - age 15-45. It is incredible right?"

"It is shocking" I confess

"Our green passport is … call it what ever you want. The present government had done too little or nothing to resolve this aching situation. This is why I personally see the need for the youth to refocus themselves into building the future. In fact, there is this youth movement building around central Europe now. A movement I believe will have its rally debut in Brussels soon"

"What is this movement all about?"

"It's an awareness movement for the youth home and abroad to take their responsibilities. A good government should be for the youth and the youth for the government but the Nigerian youth had long been forgotten. Majority of the citizens don't have any reason, no convincible reason for Mr Babangida to come back and I see no reason why he should force himself in"

"Tell me more on this youth movement and its coming up rally"

"As of last week before I flew in here, circulars were distributed around Nigerian associations and individuals around Europe to hold a meeting in Brussels. I think the meeting is to discuss organizing peaceful demonstrations in Nigerian embassies and high commissions all over Europe against IBB coming back"

"Mrs. Ediren, why do you think these demonstrations necessary in Europe?"

"I guess it is to attract the EU government on Nigeria political situation, an issue not really clear among many EU member States as presented by Obasanjo government. My own opinion is this Felix...

"Common"

"The true cure of the nation's problem would be a change of mentality..."

"Right"

"...self education on patriotism. Say for instance, Obasanjo changed! Let me clear this Felix, there is no doubt in my mind that the President have a genuine wish to see this country in progress. There should be more than a wish and hope to revive a falling giant. Perhaps if the President change, change with inverted comma, and we all, the rest citizens follow his foot steps, I would say regardless of who is ruling, Nigeria in few years will be a world-power nation. The story will be the same if we change people and not our mentality. It is going to be the same even when you say Obasanjo go and Babangida don't come! Who is going to stay... Dangote? Maybe he needs to rule for the 200 million naira investment in 1999 Obasanjo's campaign"

"We have a lot to think about"

"Yes"

"Your personal feeling about Mr Babangida"

"First, permit me to express my admiration to Mr Babangida as a strong, determined individual who had contributed in some way to Nigeria. I don't see any reason for Mr Babangida to put himself through another political turmoil with all he has achieved. Thank you and God help Nigeria"

"Hello" another call

"Hi"

"I am calling to make my contribution"

"Your call is appreciated. Would you like to tell us your name and where you calling from"

"Yes, I am Emmanuel Iweagaku, I teach sociology in Nsuka

"Right"

"I want to share my view on one of the causes of youth's deterioration in our society. I will argue that because the government has succeeded in establishing a fact that, government and citizens are parallel institutions that have nothing to do with each other and this duality of established tradition has left the youth disappointed on the system and they (the youth) exhibit their frustrations through exaggerating cultism and other anti social behaviors. Youth cultism is a sign of psychological fury on our political identity crisis. The youth is the future, any nation who abandons its youth outcast itself from future progress"

"Your argument is the youth is our hope"

"That is correct Felix..."

"But at the end the youth is as corrupt as the politicians especially the ones from abroad"

"Again I agree with you. While it might have been reasonable to expect that the politicians who lived and studied in western countries: Europe and America mostly have been much more dynamic than these uneducated generals in implementing fully economic, social rights, this has not proved to be so and the former involvement in our politics which ought to be a revival has been nothing but a cursor disappointment. And there should be new ways of cursorily screening the political individuals, an exercise that that would guarantee the constitutional admissibility prerequisites"

"Are you a kind of disappointed that the west that is lord in everything proliferates these corrupt men to us"

"Let not look for a scapegoat here. We should take our responsibility"

"But the west has responsibility in developing nations"

"You right Felix but we have to take care of ourselves. To protect rights is mainly a domestic law"

"What about when the domestic laws fails in the standard imposed by international law?"

"Yes..."

"The failure of domestic laws in individual states in Africa is obvious in every reality"

"This is the reason we youth is coming to change our way of governing. John Locke following the medieval philosophers' natural rights argued that the legitimacy of a government depends not only upon the will of the people but also upon the government's willingness and ability to protect

the individual natural rights. To achieve this Felix and I am convinced Mr Babangida will agree with me too is to postulate the Kentian duty-based system of categorical imperative; the absolute moral good which is identifiable in the exercise of the virtuous will by all rational individuals"

"Thank you for you brilliant contribution"

"Nice talking with you- bye"

"Really thank you for calling and our next call is from Ini, hello Ini"

"Hi Felix"

"Hi there"

"I am Ini Attah from Ikot-Ekpene, Akwa-Ibom"

"Go ahead Ini"

"First, I'm impressed in the way General Babangida have being listening to all contributions from the public and I hope this democratic manner continues" Mr Babangida laugh.

"I often hear president Obasanjo say the G8 should cancel our debt, yes that will be a good thing when it happens just as it has recently but it will have nothing to do with the ever increasing poverty rate, will it? The leaders are going to take the money back to Swiss anyway. If debts are cancelled and financial aids granted, it's still going to be for them. The cancellation of debts will never build roads; it won't give health care, schools, water or light. G8 priority on Africa shouldn't be charity but to spread to Africa, free-equal opportunity, not 'corrupt' government and free trade to the Western world. If debt relief and aids were the solution, 54 countries in Africa with its population of circa 800 million would have been poverty free by now. Ask Gnassingbe Eyadema of Togo and Julius Nyerere of

Tanzanian what happened to their countries with all the aid they've got. In 1974 when Zaire- now Democratic Republic of Congo's citizens were going hungry and without shelters, the later exiled Mobutu Sese Seko paid $10 million to 'watch' the historical heavy weight boxing championship between the all time pugilist Mohammed Ali and George Foreman. Most black freedom fanatics see this jest as a black thing. But I see it as his fascist persona to promote his dictatorship. Ask Obasanjo, now that G8 listed Nigeria amongst the 18 countries that benefited from the 2005's 50 billion dollars Africa debt relief. On BBC interview July 2005, Ngozi Okonji Iweala confirmed the 60% debt relief and over 25 billion dollars annual net in our oil. With all this money, a Nigerian is still under a dollar a day, we will live under a cent if people we hope to lead or revive the country insist to be paid in foreign currencies. One would ask where is the patriotism if I am paid in foreign currency to work for my own country. Chinua Achebe had always cried that Nigeria's problem is not debt or geographical issues but a failure of leadership. Our leadership must take another shape from now on to have a better future. Thank you"

"Hello" another call

"Hi"

"I am calling to support the constitutional illegibility of the ex-ex people from 1960 till date and the urgency for the senate house to go making it into an act. before Obasanjo leaves. People were saying Jakunde wanted to build the underground metro service in Nigeria but the Hausas in other to continue their monopoly in trailer business blocked him. I said Metro in Nigeria? When we don't even have a locomotive train. I beg liv stori.

A railway worker was telling me in Lagos the other day that he has not received his salary for a year or so. I looked at him in confusion, thinking how can you expect money from rail service when we don't have a train or a train route? Your leaders will go to India to buy rail materials, they will take along an accountant instead of an engineer and come back with size 24 material when what is needed is size 46. These irrelevant materials will now be heaped, abandoned somewhere till weed and bush cover them to rust. That project will never be remembered again as the remaining money breath in their foreign bank accounts. Let Babangida and all the ex, ex people respect and not resist the incoming change. Before Obasanjo leave, the constitution should be amended, forbid all ex-ex and current politicians till they are embezzlement free through this incorruptible, never hold government office, independent committee and this committee will take the place of NEC. If NEC is there but Babangida still put who he wants in office, my question is, what is NEC's function then?"

"Mr...?

"Jubril"

"You are from..."

"Okene-Kogi state"

"You saying Mr Babangida don't have right to rule Nigeria?"

"Right in this sense is a natural thing. Mr Babangida is a Nigerian and all Nigerian citizens have the right to rule the country but this right is guided by principles and eligibility: like the soon to be principles: embezzlement free in office history, education, selflessness and many others already in existence.

Not till we; me, you, Mr Babangida and every body pass these tests, the right is revoked and we are illegible to any public post"

"I am speechless on your political reformation and ideology. Are you Churchill or something?" he laughs

"I wish. I did my thesis on Rousseau; this French who defined democracy to my liking; with this natural man working in his moral grace signed in the social contract"

"I wish people like you are given a chance"

"I'm flattered"

"Thanks for calling in"

"Thank you for having me". I pick another call

"Esosa Ighodaro from Benin City hello"

"Hello"

"How are you joining us?"

"Compliment for the program"

"Thanks"

"As many callers have usefully contributed, I quite agree that our present corrupt mentality is now a tradition and custom that will soon bury the remains of Nigeria. I will say our only hope is for the youth to stop following the foot steps of our leaders, break away from this materialistic, power craziness."

"What will you like to change?"

"Above all, our mentality; the corruption that is devouring this nation in geometrical speed leaves nothing or little for Nigeria's future. No law or constitution works with corrupt minds. Whether it's the Ten Commandments

or the Sharia, it's not working. We have good laws in this country but who is obeying them? none! It is easy to put every thing on Obasanjo. Obasanjo is the head that make policies, distributes the money, yes! Is he who works at the canter in the bank? Is he who stays at the port to see the right goods come into the country? Is he who sets and marks the school examinations? Or is he the SSS that investigates crimes? Answer to the above questions is naturally no. We citizens need a change too. The change needs to start from our households to neighbors, to cities and then to the entire society. The youth has this responsibility to start teaching one another"

"Do you agree with this 30 -70years political age?"

"Of course yes, Formal military and civilians must be screen through a well organized incorruptible, youthful, never hold government office, independent commission before contesting for any public post"

"Even the civilians?"

"Why not? These new hungry civilians are worst. Mr Lucky Igbinedion for instance...the governor of my State, he has nothing to be remembered for when he leave except for mismanagement of funds and unkempt promises. As a local government chairman, he worked free for the people. This is what the paperwork said, how far is that true no one can guarantee. Right, people heard this and hope better days were coming...better days indeed! For where e! Eight years as a governor has nothing to be remembered"

"Nothing at all?"

"Oh he can...yes he can be remembered for the streets and roads he changed to his family name or his trade mark name. But I guarantee that *as soon as he leaves, someone coming in is going to wipe off these names and replace them with other names, I hope with the appropriate names.*

"But a governor will remain in history" I try to bite

"History on roads or lights or in schools, on salary or in hospital? History in what? That he sends his brothers to England with loads of moneybags that usually shocked the British authority at the port of entry. If it take me leaving my job for months to attends and be part of this demonstrations coming up in Nigeria embassies around Europe, I will be glad to do it"

"Oh you will be traveling to Europe for the events though?"

"I will be there, I lives in Netherlands"

"I see, much easier for you. Thank you for your contribution. Hello Emeka Chizo" I answer another call

"Hello"

"Emeka you're live with us in give democracy a chance. Where are you calling from?"

"From Awka- Anambra but I am a Swedish resident. When people use that word poor, poverty with inverted commas, it really pisses me off because Nigeria is not poor. It's amongst the World 50 most expensive countries to live in. Nigeria should be into industrial revolution that will put her into global marketing instead of depending on the limited resource of oil, which is mainly the nation's GDP. This will show Nigerian leaders incompetence as they rely solo on oil and abandon other valuable resources like rubber, cocoa, cassava, cotton to mention but a few. The oil industries even employ just only 100,000 people out of about around 150 million people. Government placed ban on goods without effective trade policy. These so-called men in

the custom, with their green khaki, they go to the port where goods are confiscated with confused reasons. Walking with their potbellies like a nine month pregnant woman 'That's a nice Mercedes, take it to my compound' they would order with their oga attitude. Nigerian presidents, especially Obasanjo has always had bad economic policies. Look at him in the 70s ... operation feed the nation...then again, with oil boom, he said steel mills will do the magic. Ajaokuta steel plant till today has not produced an aluminum pot. The Soviet Union that had the contract never translated their ideas from Russian to English, no one knows if the Nigeria government ever read the project at all. But all this money went to the big khaki pocket or their wide, deep boba & shokoto pockets. See the mobile phone, Obasanjo government in 2001 only, sold licenses worth 800 million dollars to private phone companies. $800 million in a year, $30 billion annual income from oil, yet naira is degrading every six hours in international market and the doom fiscal policy is not bothering the government, they don't care. This oil in 50 years might not be as valuable as it is now. In Asia, Japan for instance, is developing cars and engines that will not need fuel in the near future. Europe; Scandinavian mostly is investing fortune in bio fuel- fuel from sugar cane and weeds. G8 nations are building more nuclear plants as a solution to the increasing energy demand. So it is time to put visionaries into our government. Other countries prime ministers, presidents, ministers lobby, fight, negotiate for nuclear power, trade, research, industries but ours fight over oil, how much they can steal. Instead of taking advantage of our oil, now that, it has value. With this alarm on global warming, Scientists blames excessive gas emission; that the Greenhouse gases melting?..."

"Don't worry much about it…the scientist themselves are confused on the issue. In 1975, they told us the earth was cooling and we are heading towards the ice age now it is global warming"

"Whatever! Anyhow, what if, in fifty years the technology says we don't need oil; we've found other source of energy to replace the fossil fuel. What are you going to fight over? Have you ever sit down and think about this? This is the reason we need visionaries in the government. The latest fashion now is what you can make your country achieve and not what you can loot from your country, thank you"

"Thanks for your contribution"

"Hello" another call.

"Hi, let me put you on hold for this question" I hurry the reading from my note

"Political analysis said NEC is the copycat of FEDECO- incapable election regulator" his thrusty grin pave way to a surly silence. I will try the question again after this call

"Saliu Wahab from Ganye- Adamawa, you are live with give democracy a chance"

"Thank you Felix"

"Any contribution?"

"Yes, I would like to add to the impressive points the last caller Mr Chizo made on oil"

"Good"

"Now the demand for energy consumption is growing high; see the China increasing demand in recent years. According to the International

Energy Agency (IEA), the World consumes about 83 million barrels of oil daily; with the moment price of $70 a barrel. The oil is no longer flowing on the surface of the earth, you need special fluids to pump up the far remains and soon it will be too expensive to go down to catch this black liquid. Chevron, America second largest oil company in adverts in World leading newspapers like financial times, fears energy will be one of the crucial issues of this century. '...one thing is clear; the era of easy oil is over' they declared. Mexico has the World second largest oil field by production. Looking at the future's energy, Petroleos Mexicanos, the State oil company had begun declining in oil production...why? Maybe to find alternatives. What are Nigerian leaders doing? Fight over oil revenue allocations. God help Nigeria. Thank you"

"Thank you Mr Wahab. More to come after the break stay with us"

"Hello" I answer another call after the commercial break

"I am Femi Ladipo from Ogun State- Ijebu-Ode but I live with my family in Spain"

"Spagnolo"

"Holla"

"Welcome home gentle man"

"Thank you Felix"

"Any contribution?"

"Yah. I heard my fellow citizens on the debt cancellation issue. Well, if African leaders, especially Nigerians indeed believe that debt cancellation will solve our problem...I mean..." he laugh

"…is…" *I'm sure he can't find a word or phrase to picture what he's trying to say*

"…whoever thinks…" *he continue*

"…that white countries are going to help build our country or build Africa, that person is blind to history. Otherwise, he or she had realized that whites had never been so concerned about African than what they are going to take away from it. They will never build your country, when did they become building angels? This is why I see our leaders who carry our money meant for the people to whites' banks as the most ignorant, inferiority complexed idiots. We should let competitive-computer age minds take up our leadership, there lays our hope. Figures like Babangida should water new flowers to make a beautiful garden. South African Thabo Mbeki said '…renaissance is a sure thing to come in Africa, only when its aims are defined and guided by we Africans and taking the responsibilities for our failing government', thank you" I look at the time, it's about ten minutes to the end of the show, one more commercial and a call or two to take. Mr Kadiri hello"*

"*Hi*"

"*Profession?*"

"*Senate member from the second republic but I'm now working for NASA in America*"

"*Why did Mr Kadiri, you abandoned politics in Nigeria and take all his talent to America?*"

"*You know Felix that America is a country like nearly all western countries that rewards people by merits, that is what I lacked in Nigeria*"

"So you left because something was not right with the government?"

"Exactly, the politics was corrupt and ethnicities blinded every one"

"I can understand"

"It is so depressing even now, not a single soul in Nigeria; no exception, including myself can tell the difference between modernization and westernization. It is a fact, if you will agree with me Felix…that modernization is the wheel in which progress rotates"

"You bet I have no doubt about that"

"We Nigerians…" he continue

"…are so convinced that to progress means to westernize. In Nigeria, we think to be modern, you have to have some foreign accent, wear American jeans, party in Italian shoes or wear French perfumes without even bothering to think how they were made. Because Ramsey Noah wore that T-shirt in the movie time bomb then that is the shirt. Our artists' names must be Run DMC and the film industry must be Nollywood, not Lagos or Onitsha where these low budget movies are made. The musical videos must be like that of Eminem or 50 cent. 50cent is American culture and they are dealing with it, Nigeria has culture, we should be dealing with our own. When we come back from Europe or America, we are ashamed to speak our mother tongue because to us, we are too modern to speak in native language. The reason that, Europe and America cannot dominate Asia is that the Asians hold their identities and know the meaning of modernization. Japan for instance, sixty years ago crumbled on the feet of America when what the Roman Physicist Enrico Fermi prepared inside the Manhattan project steamed Hiroshima and Nagasaki to nothingness. But Japan is the first

non-white country to defeat a European nation-Russia. Today, Japan is the world second largest economy and, head-head in anything with the America, Britain, Canada or any world power. And their culture- their food, dressing, language are strong tower of their modernity. They came to Europe learned the European technology, went back home and modified the knowledge to their ways. Nigerians do the opposite. Now in Nigeria, you cannot say you were born in the village because the Abuja or Ikoyi guys will not pally with you. You cannot impress even a street girl except you take her to the copied McDonald's – Tantalizer or Mr Bs. Bye to our local buccal with fresh organic food; cuisine we shouldn't give up for these Western pre-package, processed fast foods with preservatives and chemicals. Well, welcome to obesity. I can't hold any mobile phone unless it's 'blue eye' camera Motorola latest. But in Japan, you will enjoy their wooden spoon Sushi food, wear their Kimono dress and ride their bullet trains, all equivalent to that of New York, London, Paris or Milan..." laughter in the audience and Mr Babangida show a participating grin.

"...no, it's not a laughing matter" Mr Kadiri voice echo bluntly through the phone speaker like a parent quenching his disturbing children in a dinner table.

"I intend not to be humorous..." he continue with a calm formal tone but the seriousness is overwhelming

"... as a matter of fact, we shouldn't laugh over this, if you want to laugh, you can go to the show 'Night of a thousand laugh' or invite Akin and Popo to entertain you" laughter again. This time, Mr Babangida joins.

"In Nigeria..." himself laughing

"...you have vending machines in Federal/State offices' lobbies just because it's like that in Oslo, in Seoul or in Montreal but our international airport roads are dark with no lights and weeds outgrown the only functioning narrow tarmac where cows blocks the landing planes. The funniest thing about these leaders is they have private mosques in their estates and park private planes inside their farms. We ruffle in the urbanity of the west- a psychological difficulties stem from repression, caused in a particular by the social avoidance strategies to which westerners had been subjected to since the industrial revolution. I would advice that we have ourselves cured, have a sober reflection before the 2007 election. I see real education (I don't mean buying certificates) to redeem us from this inferiority complex, ignorant, copy-copy lifestyle. Thank you"

"Before you go Mr Kadiri, how do you see the possibility of coming home for politics?"

"Frankly, I don't see any chance"

"Why?"

"Simply for two reasons, one because the government is till what it is, and secondly, I am outgrowing the political age the youth is advocating"

"Do you support the idea?"

"I think it will help sharpen Nigeria"

"Thank you once again Mr Kadiri for being with us"

"My pleasure"

"I look forward to get our call again"

"That will be nice... to talk with you about the West"

"What about it?" A silence reluctance grow from the other end and a keen exasperation follows

"Like I can not understand why people found British/American invasion of Iraq vague, except they failed to look back history. Historically, invasion is what the West does for a 'living'. Iraq invasion is a repeating history of when the British Prime Minister Anthony Eden in 1957 lied to his people and took the French to invade Egypt for their Suez Canal. Though Egyptian President- A. Nasser absorbed his country this time but Eden's plot beside his downfall has fuel the Israelis-Arabs feud. From a close watch of Nikita Khrushchev and Eisenhower, though not close enough for the 3rd World War. But it was enough for President Eisenhower to lure America into the Middle East affairs. A complicating politics they are now a pioneer"

"What a story"

"My point here is, the West will always take from you more than you think it will give"

"Obviously"

"J.F. Kennedy invaded Cuba in 1961 for sugar cane and tobacco. Fidel Castro had had a similar story of Saddam today if not for the Russians"

"I'm afraid we have to leave this till next and again thank you Mr Kadiri"

"Thanks Felix"

"Give democracy a chance, we will be right back". Pubblicità. The producer signal me for time off

"Welcome back" I flip pages of my questionnaire to the last page and settle for a round up. Mr Babangida had asked me during one of the

commercials breaks if we could be talking frequently... 'An honor Mr President' I had replied. He suggested a dinner talk at 08:30 post meridian the next day but my flight will be ready then. I will see. The camera zoom my face as I rearrange on my chair like a criminal lawyer concluding a two-month litigation trial. Papers spread between my two hands. My eyes look earnestly into the zoomed camera. The videographer is inches away from my table. My voice is solemn like a rookie pleading a favored verdict before unconvinced jury

"This program..." I begin with a little attention to Mr Babangida who is listening with tired look

"...is not a paint IBB black game, but a simple Patriotic-defendable effort to contribute to the solution of a motherland's progress. I don't want to identify myself as a bi partisan or a non-partisan. I am a nationalist whose cry is for a change, a change for a new start for the future of our children and our children's children. Our future will be a future without the circling friends of GENERALS, who had relegated the populace to the role of mere spectators. The same general-men in brocade had never demonstrated that Nigeria citizens are part of the government but they had only succeeded in saying government and the populace are dis-interdependent and have no common dreams or mutual interests. These army generals continue to fire gun to these loving, united citizens, evoking more recent tragedies. But the elegant people of this tormented nation would now have to re-discover their lives and more lighthearted attitude. An atmosphere of regained youth will emerge. The youth, a phenomenon the future rests on. My fellow citizens, my youth of this nation, be aware now that a vital force is ready to be formed, a

force that will bring back Nigeria into focus, competition, patriotism, balance and wealth. Time to time, people advocate decentralized government as the solution to the pejorative situation of this country. As a nationalist, I doubt that. I strongly believe that if this country is not working as a 36 state federation, there is no convincible evidence it will function better as a regional confederation or worst independent nations. Nigeria's problem is not its physicality but its people's ideological wreckage. The unintelligibility of our leaders will be carried to whatever form Nigeria becomes. 'Let divide the country' we all cry as if that will stop us from stealing. If Ibos have their country and the Hausas have theirs and the Yoruba- theirs, is it not going to be the same people?... Comrade Chukwumerije-Arthur Nzeribe Ibo, Babangida-Danjuma north or Obasanjo-Tom Ikimi west. So? '...Nigeria politicians...' (as Africa editor of the Economist: Robert Guest puts it in his book: THE SHACKLED CONTINENT) '...have at times sought to stir up rather than sooths...the governments have made laws that explicitly discriminate against their own citizens...and ethnic solidarity is used to justify Nigeria's great vice: corruption'. We are in a democracy but military is in power" I flip over the page

" This book has no intension claiming a topographical guide of Nigeria democracy. However, it can perhaps be assumed as a route map in some areas of its fundamental analytical and normative jurisprudence. A constitution will be amended to forbid the recycling ruling names and all former armies to participate in polities or hold public office till they undergo legal screenings, probes, and investigation in their office lives. Until they are cleared and with assured guarantee that they will only be part of

reconstruction and not what they have represented in history. Only then they will be constitutionally legible to contest or hold a Nigeria public office. Reconstruction is for clean hearts and anyone with dirty heart must first be cleansed before participating in reconstruction. To sanitize Nigeria of today, in the course of this desire progress, a change is needed. This change must, shall start from the recycling names of the generals. A new era will begin a real democracy in Nigeria. I'd proposed privatization in all sectors monopolize by the government. This will not only breed job efficiency, it will control corruption and promote patriotism. The senate house is urge with patriotic urgency before the Obasanjo tenure expires to amend the constitution- to have an article that forbid anybody who have held or holding government offices from Federal to local government council level to participate directly or indirectly in government office election till there is a clearance, a certificate of embezzlement free and a guarantee of a citizen worthy of serving the nation. This process will be conducted by a 36 member independent committee- each member from the 36 States including the Federal Capital. Each State has to put forward a representative in whichever form suitable for them but following the constitutional guidelines. This committee will control the electoral rules seeking advice and support from International Organizations and G8 nations - if necessary. Our new era will start from the electoral system, which is the head. What we have now in Nigeria politics is the body and the tail. There is no way we can move forward with only body and tail. You need the head. If this committee comes to existence, then we have a head; a head where eyes, ears, nose and brain are located. So let construct a youthful, incorruptible, selfless, independent, never hold government office HEAD to make a great nation we deserved. The youth are ready for this change and the time is come, acta non-verba. This is to sound a refusal for the incipient totalitarianism and any resistance from the ruling names will be a colossal error that will lead their long-term ideology into catastrophe" I take a quick look at my guest

"They should stop their lootocracy, hegemonic, quasi feudal politics in other to avoid the Guillotine that will be the memory of their rule. We will be proud to say, for our children's tomorrow, we gave our today. I'd rather die a free man than a slave. When a free man dies, he looses the pleasure of life, but when a slave dies, he looses pain. I'd rather die Dele-Giwa or Saro Wiwa than to live in opulence on the 'blood' of others. I rather cry here in the wilderness than to have seat in Abuja and dine in 'Aso-Rock' with money meant for the citizens"

I balance myself on the chair taking a little breath break

"This is the morality and dignity we youth needs to cultivate in other to have a future. I know this sound utopia to some skeptical citizens but to many visionaries, it will be a path way to real democracy. I will contribute my little to a great nation as Nigeria, I will fight for my right even when I am standing alone, for I can put up with loosing a fight but I can not stand not fighting at all. Saro Wiwa, as the loudness of silence ticked his fate of 10 November 1995, he found the spirit to leave a farewell epistle. In it, he instructed ' …literature in a critical situation such as Nigeria's cannot be divorced from politics. Indeed, literature must serve society by steeping itself in politics, by intervention, and writers must not merely write to amuse or to take a bemused critical took at society. They must play an interventionist

role ...the writer must be l'homme engage' May his soul rest in perfect peace. He said we must fight for a change and that we must not be frightened by the enormity of the task or by the immorality of the present because history will be on our side. We are to sing louder, more physically the song of Amo Tutuola, Festus Iyayi, Ben Okri, Achebe, Fela, Gani and the rest. When you read a book like the famished road, we can see in the last section of this 'spirit' book how the booker prize winner- Ben Okri transcended the main character Azaro from a pre-colonial tormenting abiku to a C21 polemic, political observer. From life beyond 'his' dad like the Biblical prophet, preached our responsibility '...we must take interest in politics' he said 'we must be spies on behalf of justice...there is no rest for the soul. God is hungry for us to grow'" I takes a breath

"This book in my plain sincerity is not a political book but an effort to make Babangida and his term generals to think it is time to stop their grievous endeavors on the expense of our future and the future of our children. Babangida is a man from grass to grace who ought to represent our hope and be a role model to the deserving majority but turned to become two things; two things he had failed to realize...his inability to a change and his inability to stop. He should stop that self-glorification and illusional grandeur in an unrepentant manner that shows his intellectual limitation. He proudly said for 'your tomorrow I gave my today' but he failed to honor that inevitable constructive criticism against his illegitimate stewardship. A leader who changes names and decrees to functions the same thing. He changed the Supreme Military Council (SMC) to Arm Force Ruling Council (AFRC) in 1985. The dissolution of Federal Executive

Council and the National Council of States to New National Council of Ministers and National Council of States (1985). The abrogation of Public Officer Decree Num. 4, the abolition of office of the chief of Staff, Supreme Headquarters and the change of Supreme Headquarters (SHQ) to General Headquarters (GHQ), Chief of General Staff (Ukiwe) with duties of political administration without control over the military. The change of ministers comprising ten civilians (Sept. 1985). The establishment of MAMSER, DFFRI, OAU Chairman Two political parties SDP and NRC, with all these and many more we had expected water from the river with a basket" my guest is listening with agony of suspect who cannot escape forensic evidence

"I can see why this England lawyer and Wale's Supreme Court solicitor Banjo Odutola called Babangida an unreliable leader, a fine soldier and strategist but an unworthy military Genera, a loyal friend to his chosen inner circle but an enemy to the dreams and aspirations of millions of his fellow citizens. Powerful players in our polities are variance to his plane, a very rich man of inexplicable wealth who lives in opulence when his governance sent millions of Nigeria citizens into adjacent poverty. And one thing he failed to realize is that when you have a good intention for your country you don't need to rule a country to achieve so much for your fellow citizen. He should learn from Obasanjo who is convincingly unprepared and inappropriate to the first Nigeria position despite his earlier experience as a head of State. This only proves that military dictatorship is different from democratic rule. A military dictatorship, which only is known to Babangida and democratic rule, he knows not. He will soon found this

out but on the expense of our nation and we poor citizens who continue to suffer undeservedly for his bad rule and sequential influenced rules. The nation should fight her freedom from Babangida before we fall into his anarchy. If he say he can use letter bombs to take our heritage form us, then we are left with nothing than to use the love of that heritage; a nature that describe our freedom. Our first step is to gain the ability to face our goal. Our difficulty will prevail if we continue to stay in the compound of our cowardice. And we must remember this; the future can never be bright to those who cannot confront it. We will stand up and block his 'must' way to Aso-Rock. The queue will be long; he might shoot and kill till his bullets will be used up. We will weaponlessly hold him and hug him with our motherland's hearts. We will bathe him and join him in the queue to be amongst us...his brothers. We will make him a belonger of Nigeria nation and not the owner of it... God help Nigeria. Babangida who had mistook his heroism for immortality and refused to understand that popularity is not the same as sainthood and he keep failing to understand and greedily can not accept the fact despite..." what he is hearing is giving way to his emotion. I can see it through his sobering eyes

"*...obvious reasons he lack the temperament to operate in a democratic setting.*

Apart from a democracy is the government by the people... it is also and more equals to a system of government, which thrives on compromises. Col. Umar sees compromise to Babangida as a strange bedfellows and antithetical to his military beliefs. Babangida is a man who 'outwitted Nigerians, embezzled funds, canceled free and fair election, made mess of people's civil rights, killed and murdered people in cold blood yet walk freely in our streets and now some hungry idiots keep singing lord to his name. He backstabbed us into dark days. His junta was the highest junk age that forced our youth to Europe and America to slave...our boys duplicating bankcards and our girls losing their womanhood dignity. He is now custoding presidential files that ought to be historical materials for our nation in national treasury. Only weak intellectual person could lack such sense of patriotism of taking historical files into his personal custody. He destroys the trust citizens have for their nation. Mr Babangida popularly known as Nigeria 'Maradona'. This name was invented by late Chief Bisi Onabanjo...Maradona borrowed from the Argentina born world soccer hero who built his legacy apart from his tactical wizardry in the green pit, he injusto scored a world cup goal with his hand. Since then, Maradona in Nigeria has be a metaphor for cheat, outlaw, cunning and the rest negative characteristics of mankind. This is Babangida who now have big say in all high nocturnal meetings. He chairman every obscure book lunch and ever presents in social parties and political funerals. He continue to promote the capitalist ruling class of this nation with their opportunist characteristic that continue to compromise anything in order to maintain the greedy, poor in mind, arrogant, oppressive capitalist system that strengthens the godfatherism (a traditional cake everybody is striving to have a piece of). During Babangida regime, Nigeria bureaucratic, political and judicial processes were put up for rent, when corruption became a virtue and a tradition that eroded the quality of public services. And access to those services and the result has been political and economic benefit flow to limited individuals while the cost continues to rest on the heads of the poor and the powerless. Under Babangida, corruption assumed a new dimension; it became a fundamental policy since independence. The obvious corrupt Babangida government had abused public trust and attacked the very foundations of collective national existence and injured the vital interest of the nation and its' people. Babangida had failed to respect Nigeria fundamental constitutional laws... like the 1999 constitution that require the president and all other high ranks of his offices to declare their assets and pledge to abide by national code of conduct. Chapter two of the constitution obliges the president all his high rank assistance to promote and realize the security and welfare of the Nigerian citizens including their freedom and happiness. The chapter obligates the president and his assistance to prevent exploitation of Nigerian's human and natural resources for any reasons other than for the good of the community. With this Babangida failed and had not since proven himself different from his old self. This is the fear of his coming back. International human rights law requires any one responsible for human rights violations to be judge and the victims obtain remedy for damage suffered and not until this is done in Nigeria by Obasanjo government, Babangida is not qualify to contest in any Nigeria public office and if he tries to act contrary as he has always does, he will be meeting the veto power of the sovereign...the citizens. Babangida abused Nigeria human rights...(see the definition of human rights as define by the UN General Assembly 'Magna Carta for Victims' of 29 November 1985) and not until Babangida clears himself from this, his leadership in whatever form will be illegitimate. Except he is brought to justice promptly and fairly, he is not legible to any government office and Obasanjo government lacks credibility not only to the Nigerians at home and abroad but also to the international communities. In other to protect the fragile democratization process of this nation, we must do some thing as a Nation, groups, individual against the continuity of impunity being enjoyed by Babangida and his team. Impunity has now been traditionalized with money and every corrupt politician is written in the album of impunity. No wonder the innocent Nigerian youth now engage in anything that will yield money in other to see their names in the album of impunity; poor sours who now lives with their ideological wreckage. People should be ready for a change. A change I am convinced will never come easily" My guest is following with more relax and interesting look but his physical stiffness tells different. His eyelash bristle and his manicure fingers claw the absolvent in his left hand.

"We have to be ready..." I continue

"...to confront powerful interest groups that clearly benefits from the political monopoly that will resist any such of mental revolution I am advocating. The fight should not and will not be of tripartite division amongst the Hausa-Fulani north, the Igbo-east and the Yoruba-west. It will have nothing to do with the south-south geo-political stuffs. It will be one Nigeria effort to put who is right...Hausa, Igbo, Yoruba, Edo, Calabar in the position he or she will fits and he or she will work hard for the interest of the nation. It won't be the ethnical rotation of power. I don't care if an Hausa man rules as a president for twenty years, I'm careless if an Igbo woman be the vice president for thirty years. It won't bother me if a Yoruba or any south-south man or woman being a president for years. My care, my

hope, my dream is a man or woman to rule with the democratic qualities and he or she will fight for us- our values, our gains, our interests, our social rights and economical benefits. He could rules as long as the constitution allows...'why changing leadership if he is going good and he is pushing the nation into prosperity' the Sydney residents said of John Howard after he won his fourth term as the Australian Prime Minister (Oct. 2004). There is so much Mr Babangida is unaware of, how would he think it is appropriate to leave this country in his hand at the moment we need to put our heads together. We need some one who know our problems, one who is current of the present situation and who have vision of bringing back the nation to its' cause. We all should be ready to sacrifice and have our nation back. And we need Babangida to play a very important role that would make him our hero. He knows who is worth to rule this country. He should support them, giving them autonomous chance to work while he assists as a father. We will all hold our hands to build this nation because we have no other one. We will come out to have our nation back. A nation will hand over to our children and our children's children. A nation where democracy will be practice in full and we will resume our old name the giant of Africa. We will have a nation where University students prefer to reseat their failed exams and not to 'block' with the lecturers. We will have a nation where we no longer run to abroad to crack... and prostitute in the streets of Italy and Frankfort. We will live in a nation where we will sing our national anthem in our hearts. It will then be a nation where people serve their nation and not themselves. We will live in a nation where production is amply rewarded and surplus and left over will be uncountable. We will live in a nation where every body works for the general will and not the individual will. We will have citizens who Nigeria will call and they will obey, we will then live in a nation where every body will serve their mother's land with love, strength and faith, so that our heroes' services will never be in vain. We will live in a nation bounds with freedom and not of ethnic conflicts, marginalization or revenue sharing imbalance. We will live in a nation where we will stand to say this is our country to which we will sacrifice our lives a thousand times. My grievance against our leaders is of disillusionment and not of resentment, for these I say, I say not from my selfish self but for the hopefulness of my motherland, God help Nigeria" I raise my head from the questionnaire and gaze into the camera.

"This nation has given me her trust and this trust has call for a duty to service. I have taken the duty to serve my beloved country and any road I take on this course will surely lead me back home. I am ready to die before I wake up, but let someone wakes when I die. This is my truth, you may take it as a lie for an American president once said '…whoever fears no truth needs fear no lies'" I look up from my reading and face my guest

"Thank you Mr President for coming and il boca lupo to you" he nods and I face the camera

"That's all from us this week, do tune in prossimamente and thanks for watching. God help Nigeria"

ABOUT THE AUTHOR

VESCOVI Ogunsuyi Felix was born on September 11th 1971 in Benin City-Southern Nigeria. Felix studied cinema in Italy and behavioral Science at Open University England. He worked as an independent columnist in many Italian local newspapers. He also worked with the Italian immigration as interpreter and cultural intermediator. He is the president and founder of 'MIRROR de afro' (an NGO which promotes Nigeria image in European Union territories). Other of his books: Daydreaming, Hard Through, How we were, Seek pleasure.